blue cuban nights

ted ferguson

SUMMERSDALE

Summersdale Publishers Ltd
46 West Street
Chichester
West Sussex
PO19 1RP
UK

www.summersdale.com

Printed and bound in Great Britain.

ISBN 1 84024 226 4

about the author

Ted Ferguson is an award-winning author and journalist who has published hundreds of magazine and newspaper articles and six non-fiction books. He has travelled widely in Asia and the Middle East and, after living for several years in England and Mexico, now makes his home in Toronto.

To Frances Hanna, for soldiering on

contents

chapter one

The man sitting behind me had a problem. He had forgotten to set the timer on his VCR before driving to the airport and now, 30,000 feet above the Florida Keys, he was worried about missing a comedy special.

'Have they got HBO in Cuba?' he asked the flight attendant. 'Can I get it at the hotel?'

'I don't know, sir,' the woman replied. 'You might be able to.'

'Could you find out for sure?' the man pressed. 'I hate going anywhere not knowing what to expect. The travel agent said there was cable, but he didn't say there was HBO.'

While the flight attendant went to the front of the aircraft, presumably to investigate the television situation, I stared out of the window at a group of rumpled white clouds and wished missing a comedy special was all I had to concern me. For the first time in my life, I was bringing contraband into a foreign country. I could claim some of the items in the suitcase – the half-dozen tins of salmon, the Spanish-language books, the jeans and shirts – were for my personal use, but the customs inspectors were unlikely to accept that explanation for the children's underwear and the '56 Chevy spark plugs. If I was caught, there was a good chance they'd just confiscate the goods and warn me against trying it again. A good chance, but not a certainty. Cuba was a dictatorship, and I could be getting myself into serious trouble.

The baggage handlers were another worry. At the country's biggest airport, José Martí, luggage locks are picked and the contents pilfered with impressive speed. A friend of mine gratefully discovered his thieving handler was a person of modest needs: he passed up the silk ties and Gucci shoes and stole a couple of 'Golf Or Die' T-shirts. I remember a British traveller saying he was on an aircraft waiting to depart when he noticed a handler grab a suitcase off a cart near a 747, run across the tarmac and throw it over a wall. But that was Havana and I was flying into Holguín, a small and hopefully less criminally inclined city near the east coast.

The flight attendant returned. She told the man behind me that the pilot had stayed at the same hotel, but as he hadn't watched television he couldn't say which cable services were available. When she left, the man said to the woman seated beside him, 'I'm wondering if this is a real big mistake. What am I going to do? Lie on the bloody beach?'

I didn't have to look at Jessie, my wife, to know she was smiling. Lying on the beach was her paradise found. She had collected a hodgepodge of novels, Nadine Gordimer associating with Amy Tan, Ian McEwan bumping up against Pat Conroy, and she planned to read them in an oceanside lounge chair every chance she got.

We had been coming to Cuban beaches for ten years, Canadians running from ice and snow and painful temperatures like panicky civilians fleeing Godzilla's hostile presence. But Cuba represents more than going to a beach for me, more than just exchanging northern darkness for southern light. I grew up in a home totally empty of love, humour and appealing conversation in a country where politeness and dispassion are considered supreme virtues. Cubans think those attitudes are unnatural. They either like you or hate you on first meeting, and they seldom hesitate to reveal which verdict they've reached. Talking is a national obsession: put two Cubans together and they'll hold a party. Family life, laughter and indigenous music are highly valued, perhaps more now than ever because of the economic horrors torturing the island. When I was at José Martí Airport two summers ago, I heard a man who had been teaching in the country say something that stuck in my mind. 'There are bad apples in every bunch,' he said to a tourist standing in the passport line, 'but most Cubans are really great people.'

Fear of losing my luggage to a bad apple or having the airline accidentally send it to Uzbekistan had long since committed me to the practice of never taking anything on a journey that I couldn't carry on board. Travelling to Cuba this time, however, it was necessary to cart along a large suitcase and, realising the airline would insist upon stowing it in the plane's underbelly, I played the Bono card. Whenever the rock singer walked urban streets dressed in a designer jacket, he attracted a lot of attention; on a trip to Toronto he sauntered along busy Queen Street wearing ageing leather and Levi's and nobody seemed to notice him. So, to increase the odds of baggage handlers and customs officers ignoring my luggage, I placed the contraband in a grubby grey suitcase I had bought for $5 at a garage sale.

The plane landed in Holguín.

I descended the portable stairs and crossed the tarmac. A coastguard helicopter, old enough to be one bolt away from metal fatigue death, sat nearby. Soldiers with tinted glasses and holstered pistols stood outside the terminal watching the disembarking passengers. In the boarding lounge, a trio of happy-faced musicians shook maracas and sang 'Guantanamera', while Canada-bound tourists, holidays over, looked as though they were being exiled to an iceberg, which, of course, they were.

The incoming passengers gathered their luggage and lined up in a small, hot air-famished room. I lifted my heavy suitcase onto a wooden table. The customs men were opening one bag in every twenty or so and waving the rest of the luggage owners through. My suitcase went untouched.

Outside, my wife and I climbed on to the air-conditioned bus heading to our hotel at Guardalavaca Beach, ninety minutes away.

Christopher Columbus wrote that Cuba possessed 'such marvellous beauty that it surpasses all other countries in charms and graces.' Proceeding east, passing green hills and acres of high sugar cane, the light softening as the sky prepared for night, that claim seemed indisputable. But there was sadness to the beauty. Some farm workers wore tattered clothing and lived in simple concrete dwellings that were a modest improvement over the Ciboney Indian huts Columbus saw in 1492. And, a fretful sign that the country was greeting the twenty-first century with a backward slide towards the 1800s, there were people all over the highway, walking from village to village, riding horses, seated in ox-drawn carts. Maimed by petrol rationing and spare parts shortages, the rural bus service was sporadic. Rather than submit to the government-approved alternative – paying a few pesos to stand in the back of one of the crowded farm trucks that bump and lurch and sway between outlying communities – hundreds of people were journeying under their own steam.

'Welcome to Cuba,' the tour company rep said into a microphone as we rolled towards the Atlantic. 'My name is Jorge. I understand that it is difficult for you to pronounce, so you can call me George. Let me tell you about Cuba. If you have any questions, I will try to answer them. Cuba is the largest island in the Caribbean. Our population is eleven million. Our yearly mean temperature is twenty-five degrees Celsius – what's that sir? No, I'm sorry. I don't know if you can get HBO at the hotel.'

Two days after we arrived at the resort, I took a Bible out of my suitcase. Someone in Toronto had asked me to give it to a hotel employee he'd met the previous winter. I'd told him I was reluctant to do it. I hadn't gone to church since childhood, and I believed it would require more than prayer to end Cuba's financial nightmare. The American blockade was crippling the island, I'd said, not a lack of Bibles. He'd successfully argued that if a woman living in an oppressed society could find comfort in a holy book, I shouldn't deny her the pleasure.

My wife entered the room. 'Are you checking the suitcase again? I thought you said the baggage handlers didn't steal anything.'

'I'm not checking. I'm going to look for the Bible lady today.'

Jessie opened the safety-deposit box burrowed in the wall. She had bought some peanuts at the lobby shop and was locking the change away. 'I can't understand why you were worried about telling customs the truth. If you'd explained that you were bringing gifts, they wouldn't have said a word.'

'They might've wanted names and addresses.'

'You're catching the Cuban disease. Paranoia.'

'I'm not paranoid. Cubans consorting with foreigners are suspicious characters. The police and the army are everywhere. Neighbours watch neighbours. Everybody reports on everybody else.'

'Miguel and Rosa aren't overly concerned. They encourage us to stay at their place.'

'Maybe there've been repercussions they haven't mentioned. Miguel did say somebody listens in on his phone calls. His letters to us are carefully worded because the police probably open them. He's a poet, and poets aren't to be trusted.'

'You could be right. Maybe the customs would've demanded names. But I'm not as paranoid as you, and I really doubt it.'

We went to the beach, a broad ribbon of sand in front of the hotel. Although the law stipulates that Cubans cannot be denied access to any beach, they knew they weren't wanted and favoured another spot half a mile south. Held hostage by their own anxieties, many tourists never stepped past the white sand and hotel grounds. Cuba was relatively safe compared to other global resorts; petty thievery happened, but violent assaults against travellers were extremely rare. Either the hotel guests didn't understand this, or something else was restricting their movement. Perhaps it was the dread of witnessing the misery that, according to American media hawks, was vast and shocking, making Cuba the Calcutta of the Caribbean. If that was the reason for their self-imposed confinement, it wasn't a legitimate fear. Every day bleak-eyed adolescents stood at the edge of a vacant lot close to the hotel entrance, selling intimacy for the price of a chocolate bar and a Coke. But no one in the nearby community was begging, no one was sleeping in the streets, and there wasn't a single hustler pushing Lada keyrings or Castro-on-velvet paintings.

As Jessie read a novel, I reclined on a plastic chair and watched the beach scene. Volleyball players were leaping and whooping, booze devotees were chain-drinking Cuba Libres, a ponytailed blonde in a lime-green bikini was helping an exhausted windsurfer raise a fallen sail. After a while, I picked up the Bible, strolled to the patio bar and asked a waiter where I could find Clara. He pointed at a woman beside the equipment shack on the beach. Clara was the ponytailed blonde.

Walking up to her, I said, 'I ran into a schoolteacher in Toronto who asked me to bring you this. It's in Spanish.'

Clara was kneeling on the sand, examining a scuba tank. She jumped to her feet, beaming as if I was handing her the deed to a Miami condo. 'Thank you, thank you. This is fantastic.'

'Getting Bibles must be a problem. Castro has been fighting the Vatican for forty years.'

'Forty-one. And I'm not Catholic.'

'Oh. I thought everyone on the island was Catholic. Except for the atheists in the Communist Party.'

'I'm in an evangelical group. Most of us used to be Witnesses. You aren't one, are you?'

'A Jehovah's Witness?'

'Yes.'

'No. I'm surprised they're in Cuba. Is that a recent development?'

'They've been here since the fifties. The government sticks them in jail, and sometimes villagers throw stones and beat them, but the Witnesses keep hunting converts.

Like hungry animals.' She folded her arms, pressing the Bible against her chest. 'I quit when a Witness refused to take her son to the hospital for blood. She let him die. I believed in the Witnesses' teachings and I was sure I could accept it. But I couldn't. I'm a typical Cuban. I adore children too much.'

The following morning, my wife and I took a taxi into Holguín.

We rode into a suburb, down narrow streets rimmed by shabby brick and concrete houses. Curious children swarmed around the taxi when it stopped at Miguel and Rosa's home; people stared from doorways and open windows. One of those gawkers, I thought, probably belonged to the Committee for the Defence of the Revolution, the national neighbourhood body that reported unusual activities to a central office. Foreigners visiting a Cuban family was certainly unusual.

Miguel greeted me with a large grin and a crushing hug. He was tall for a Cuban, well over six foot, with thin grey hair and a bony, friendly face. He was honest, even-tempered and compassionate.

I believed everything Miguel ever told me except for the story about his dead grandparents. He said their spirits had appeared when he was alone in a public square one dark night. His grandfather hovered above the bench Miguel was occupying while his grandmother waved from across the square. The couple couldn't stand being around each other for the last twenty years of their lives, he'd said, and even in death they refused to visit their grandson together.

'Rosa lost your letter and I said she shouldn't worry, you were coming this morning,' Miguel said, taking the garage-sale suitcase from my hand. 'My memory is terrible, but I don't forget important dates. My God, you're only staying a few days. You must have enough things in here for two years!'

Miguel's father had been a prosperous merchant before the Batista regime fell in 1959. A former family maid actually lived on the same street where Miguel and Rosa now inhabited a small flat-roofed house. Inside, the only vestige of Miguel's parent's pre-Fidel affluence was a broken Art Deco clock made of pink marble that the family couldn't afford to get repaired. The furniture was plain. A Cuban flag and several plaster replicas of tropical fruit hung on the walls. Jessie and I were to spend three nights in a tiny alcove off the living room where Miguel normally wrote poetry and hacked away at the forest of paperwork he lugged home from his government office.

'Angelita won't be growling at you anymore,' he said, depositing the suitcase in the alcove. 'She's on a farm.'

Rosa swept in from the kitchen, a delicate, energetic woman, as pretty in her fifties as she must have been in her twenties. She kissed Jessie and embraced me and said, 'Angelita went crazy. She stared at the door and howled. I caught her standing on the kitchen table barking. For no reason, barking. Crazy, crazy.'

'We gave her to Rosa's nephew,' Miguel said. 'He's half-mad himself. They get along fine. Birds of a feather.'

I was pleased to be rid of Angelita. She was a skeletal, big-toothed mongrel with an aching lust to disable anyone who wasn't a family member. Whenever Miguel's friend, José, drove to a distant town, he borrowed the dog to discourage thieves from pillaging his vehicle. Car parts are so scarce that even the critically wounded hubcaps from his '56 Chevy are objects of desire.

'Sit down,' Rosa said. 'I'll make coffee. Everyone will be dropping by later.'

They came all day long. Cousins, uncles, aunts, friends, Miguel and Rosa's married daughters with their husbands and their children. All for short stays and lively talk that avoided politics as if it were a toxic virus that spread through conversation. I heard the gossip. Lourdes was pregnant and had no husband; Ramón and Ana were divorcing; Miguel's brother in Santiago de Cuba was hospitalised for depression; Eduardo was an announcer at a local radio station.

Vicente showed up late in the afternoon. Rangy and good-looking, he had a huge stock of charm and confidence. He slept in a brick shed in the backyard, his way of giving Miguel and Rosa more privacy. Their son's inability to secure a permanent job was a source of anxiety for his parents, a condition that worsened when he had declared two months earlier that he planned to marry his girlfriend in the spring.

'Last month was good,' Vicente told us while his parents cooked dinner. 'I made five American dollars. Not bad, heh?'

I nodded in agreement. The average Cuban salary was the equivalent of three US dollars a month. Doctors and lawyers were paid between fourteen and sixteen dollars.

'How did you do that?' Jessie asked.

'Black market. Father despises me doing it – you know what a Party man he is – but he's stopped complaining because he knows there's nothing else I can do. He doesn't want me to be one of those guys sitting in the square talking and talking about sailing a raft to Florida or marrying a rich German girl.'

'So it's German girls these days,' I said. 'It was Swedish blondes a few years ago.'

'Swedish girls don't fly here as much as they did. Plenty of Germans, Spaniards, Mexicans and Venezuelans. Thousands of Canadians and British. The odd Russian and Bulgarian. Sometimes a Cuban will marry a foreigner and the bureaucrats still make it hard for him. A wedding licence isn't an automatic passport.'

'I'm glad you didn't do that,' Jessie said. 'Those sort of relationships hardly ever work out. Covenants with regret.'

Vicente laughed. 'I'm glad too. I've seen my friends tie themselves to women so ugly that if a snake bit them, it would be poisoned. No, I'm staying in Holguín and marrying Nena.'

'Come and eat,' Rosa called from the kitchen.

'Nena wants babies,' Vicente said. 'I do too, but I won't be completely happy. How can I be? Their food will be rationed. They'll be dressed in the old clothing Nena gathers from friends. Old diapers too. Ones her cousin put on her baby. A man should be able to provide the very best for his children. Not old diapers and somebody else's worn-out clothing.'

We had chicken for dinner. Rosa's farmer cousin contributed the bird and a relative across town supplied home-made orange wine. Both were a treat for the family, who ate rice and beans almost everyday. When Rosa apologised for not having dessert, I went to the suitcase. I hadn't informed them that I'd be leaving the bag and its treasure behind. Before booking the trip, Jessie and I debated whether or not we should bring anything. Poverty hadn't destroyed Miguel and Rosa's pride. Would we embarrass them by acting like Lord and Lady Bountiful, distributing favours upon the underprivileged? We finally agreed that although they might be momentarily embarrassed, it would be ridiculous not to extend a helping hand when it was so easy for us to obtain things. We collected novels, clothing, tinned food, medicine, toothpaste, and, a great acquisition, two copies of a medical guide.

'That looks good,' Vicente said as I carried a cellophane package into the kitchen. 'What is it?'

'Those rich German girls love these more than they love Cuban boys,' I said. 'Werther's candies.'

That night, long after my wife fell asleep, I lay in bed listening to the neighbourhood. Afro-Cuban music, a barking dog, laughing men passing the house, a rooster whose screwed-up internal timepiece was telling it that dawn was breaking. In the dark alcove, under a sun-faded photograph of Che Guevara, I lay thinking of Vicente's future babies, the broken Art Deco clock, and meals where a skinny chicken and home-made wine are special treats.

I knew more about Cuba than most foreigners – I read Cuban novels, I saw Cuban films and I subscribed to the official government newspaper, *Granma* – but I really didn't know all that much. Even with the visits to Miguel and Rosa's house, I felt like I was peering into an enormous room through a crack in the wall. I wanted to travel the island, to break out of the tourist bubble and learn everything I could about the place where, unlike any other nation, Communism moved to a rumba beat.

chapter two

Six months later I was riding in the back of a turquoise Plymouth, bouncing and rattling down Havana's seafront boulevard, en route to one of the city's most fashionable neighbourhoods. Cuban cabinet ministers and foreign diplomats were comfortably settled in Miramar mansions and, it was rumoured, Castro possessed three houses there. (Past assassination attempts persuaded Castro to frequently switch domiciles; Cubans say he sleeps in fifty different dwellings across the island.)

The car I was travelling in was a miracle of mobility. The petrol line leaked, the spark plugs skipped a beat and the tailpipe emitted a despairing amount of dense smoke, yet it kept advancing, a Sly Stallone of automobiles, valiantly determined to complete its mission. Two or three miles up the Malecón, the springs beneath the balding seat cover felt like they were digging trenches in my flesh. I slid over to the other side, away from the open window and an entrancing view of the flat, blue sea. Exhaust fumes rose from a six-inch hole near my feet. I stuck a foot over the hole but it failed to block the fumes. It was impossible to roll the window down; the handle was missing. I returned to the springs. *We'll soon be there*, I promised my miserable bum. *It won't be much further*.

Up front, Carlota and the driver were machine-gunning sentences at each other. Havana natives speak Spanish faster than rural Cubans, perhaps faster than Spanish people anywhere on earth. When they are really going at it, Berlitz immersion grads, an army of conversational phrases camped in their heads, find themselves summoning the same expression over and over: *'Por favor habla mas despacio.'* ('Please speak more slowly.')

Carlota was Rosa's friend. I had met her in Holguín, and she and her son, Roberto, had been advising me where to go and who to contact in Havana. All I knew about the bald and wrinkled motorist was his first name, Juan, and the fact that he had a house in the area near Carlota's flat. In exchange for the lift, she was rewarding him with a container of petrol Roberto had obtained somewhere in exchange for stockings and a fish.

'Do you understand?' Carlota asked, turning her head. 'I'm telling Juan that Raúl has divorced me. He moved in with that cross-eyed lesbian fifteen years ago, and he thinks it's time to marry her. Divorce is easy in Cuba. You go to a government office and fill in papers. Cuba runs on American dollars. The cafés, the hotels, the black market. Dollars, dollars. A divorce costs eighty pesos. Less than one American dollar. Cuba craves American money. It should pass a law allowing foreigners to divorce here. Charge a special fee, maybe five dollars. Can you get a divorce in Canada for five dollars? No, it costs more doesn't it? I don't need a fortune-teller to predict it. Ten, twenty, flights a day, loaded with passengers despising the creatures they married.'

When I phoned my wife in Toronto from my hotel, she was sceptical of my plan to take Carlota to lunch at a pricey Miramar restaurant. She agreed that in examining various aspects of Cuban life for my book, I ought to observe the upper heights of the economic scale, and as Carlota hadn't been to a restaurant for ten years, it would be wonderful for her to have a really good meal. But Jessie was afraid that for all the cockiness she displayed in her own neighbourhood, Carlota would walk into La Ferminia, see how fancy everything was and lose her confidence.

'Don't be surprised if she stops talking,' Jessie said. 'She could go into a shell and not come out till she's outside again. What do you know about this place?'

'La Ferminia? It's popular with foreigners on expense accounts. Fifty-dollar lobster dinners. Cigars and port.'

'Gawd, you'll be lucky if she only seizes up. She might faint and pull the table over.'

Juan guided the Plymouth through a tunnel beneath the Almendares River and we emerged in Miramar. Dotted amongst the colonial mansions were embassies, a Fiat dealership, Benetton and Cardin outlets. Juan had said he knew the restaurant's location but he was mistaken. He drove up and down streets, asked people for directions. We saw no identifying sign; nobody Juan questioned had heard of La Ferminia. It was as though the proprietors were hiding the restaurant from us, maintaining an exclusive preserve for their more prosperous clientele.

'This is ridiculous,' Carlota said. 'We can't drive and drive. We'll miss lunch. Do you know the Colonel's? Take us there, Juan.'

The Colonel's wasn't Colonel Sanders, it was her name for Mi Bohio, a tiny café operated by a retired military officer. Hundreds of humbly furnished eateries had sprouted in the city in response to the government's loosening of private-ownership rules in 1994. All of the establishments shared a common condition: the state forbade them to hire non-relatives. Consequently, the ex-army officer's staff included his wife, his daughter, his son-in-law and a changing assortment of cousins and nephews. Juan explained this to us when he parked two blocks north of the restaurant. He was leery of depositing a foreigner at its door. Private citizens suspected of accepting cash for transporting tourists were competing against state-operated taxis and had their licence plates confiscated for three months.

'I'll stay with the car,' Juan said. 'If the police say, "Why are you here?" I'll say, "The car won't start. The carburettor's sick."'

Mi Bohio translated as My Hut, but far from being a hut, the Colonel's establishment was located in his spacious house. The backyard patio of the turn-of-the-century mansion held twelve tables. There was room for more, but the government, limiting competition for the restaurants it operated, enforced a twelve-table regulation.

Most of the tables were filled. Carlota wore her best outfit, a blue dress and a fake leather belt with a gold-coloured buckle. The dress was old and when she raised her arm, I noticed a cigarette burn on the cuff. A handsome, silk-shirted man in the same age-range as Carlota, between fifty and fifty-five, sent an 'I'm-intrigued' glance in her direction. With her long, pointed nose and broad mouth she wasn't half as attractive as his dining companion, but Carlota owned qualities life hadn't awarded the young blonde – an aura of strength and sensuality.

Unintimidated by the surroundings, Carlota informed the waiter she'd like an off-menu item.

'I'm sorry, señora,' he said. 'We don't have any shrimp today.'

'You have lobster?'

'No, not today.'

'What kind of fish do you have?'

'None. We aren't permitted to sell fish.'

'Today, or ever?'

'Ever.'

'All right. I understand.' Perusing the menu again, she said to me, 'I'll be content with anything, so long as it isn't *sopa de gallo*.'

'What's that?'

'"Rooster" soup, the street name for a famous Cuban speciality. It's a mixture of brown sugar and water. We eat it in the neighbourhood whenever the cupboard's bare.'

'Sugar and water? You've got to be joking.'

'It makes a mother weep to feed her hungry child *sopa de gallo*. Children are flowers. They need good nourishment to grow. Meat nourishes them. We adults need meat too, for our health. So Cubans eat practically any meat they can lay their hands on. Did Roberto tell you the zoo story?'

'No, he didn't.'

'Birds were disappearing from cages during the night at Havana Zoo. So the government posted a security guard on the grounds. One night, a big iguana – four feet long – disappeared. The director called the guard to his office. The guard was baffled by how the thief did it. He denied he was sleeping. The director was suspicious. He called the guard back to his office three days later and interrogated him for hours. The guard finally confessed. He killed the iguana and took it home for a family feast.'

'The guard must've been fired.'

'Worse,' she said grimly. 'This is Cuba. He was executed.' Then she grinned and said, 'I don't know what happened. He's probably guarding an ant hill in the Baracoa

Mountains. You know, to stop the red ants attacking the black.'

The waiter took our orders. A couple in their thirties sauntered onto the patio and seated themselves at the table adjacent to ours. His Gap shirt looked new; her pearl earrings looked real. A grey thought clouded Carlota's face. I recognised that expression; it was common to Cubans. In an environment dense with secret police agents and true-believer citizens eager to report anti-Communist tendencies, the risk of being overheard by strangers induced wary looks and careful dialogue. There would be no more lunch table conversation pertaining to children consuming brown sugar soup and guards stealing iguanas.

'Rosa told me you were a dancer,' I said.

'Yes, when I was young I was with the Ballet de Cuba. Alicia Alonso was the soul of our company. In her sixties she was dancing *Giselle*. Almost blind. Her cataracts were so bad technicians placed bright lights on the stage so she would know exactly where she was.'

'An extraordinary woman.'

'All Cuban women are extraordinary. Our men are giant *machos* and lord it over their women in public. Scratch the surface and you will see that a woman's status in the home is more important than a man's because our women nurture our children. Motherhood rules supreme. The husband orders his wife around in other ways, but for the raising of children the husband accepts his wife's opinions. If he doesn't, the marriage flounders.'

Carlota's marital problems had nothing to do with raising Roberto. Her husband cheated on her. Carlota tried to expel the mistress from his life by employing a widely practised custom – she wrote the woman's name on a piece of paper and stashed it in the refrigerator. But the refrigerator curse didn't succeed, and her husband deserted her and Roberto for the short-haired, flat-chested office clerk she always referred to as The Lesbian.

'I don't know the exact number, but something like one in every two marriages ends in divorce. Why? Many reasons. The husband has no job, or the wife hates his machismo attitudes. One of the biggest reasons is that the vast majority of young people can't afford apartments and houses of their own. Living with in-laws for years and years brings despair and arguments. Despair and arguments bring divorce.'

After a $10-a-person lunch of roast pork, salad and chocolate cake, we strolled to the rendezvous point. The Plymouth's bonnet was up and Juan was studying the engine. Cuban vehicles were mostly Detroit antiques, Dodges and Chevys, Oldsmobiles and Nashes, painted red, yellow or aquamarine. Mechanical problems were so commonplace that a raised car bonnet ought to have been the national symbol, printed on stamps, flags and sporting event logos.

As we approached the Plymouth, Juan slammed the bonnet down and said, 'Quick, jump in the car. The motorcycle police were here.'

'This is ridiculous,' Carlota said under her breath. 'I cry for Cuba. The police are smothering her.'

We rattled and bounced through the tunnel to the Malecón. A black freighter was heading into port, flying a Costa Rican standard. Juan told Carlota he was repairing a friend's bathroom plumbing in exchange for clothing. Carlota urged Juan to visit her fortune-teller, an 87-year-old spinster whose whispery predictions often came true. I sat quietly in the back, a victim of the springs.

Juan dropped me several blocks from my hotel. I wanted

to walk, to get a stronger sense of what it was like to live in the utterly bewitching – and sadly decaying – city.

Havana. The name rolls off the tongue like vintage cognac. Havana. The name implies romance, raucous music, heat, the scent of bougainvillea, the taste of minty drinks, a hedonistic bent that even Communism cannot straighten. The name of the British Columbian city where I grew up had no such connotations. Victoria had a firm, joyless sound to it. Like the rigid monarch the city was named after, the residents embraced pious respectability. They went for tea and crumpets in Government Street cafés, studied the history of the British Empire in schools, exhibited roses and chrysanthemums at horticultural fairs. Tudor- and Elizabethan-style houses peppered solid-sounding communities like Oak Bay and the Uplands. The local newspaper of record was a stodgy publication called *The Daily Colonist*; the paper's best-known columnist was a lean, pipe-smoking fellow who, emulating British writers, used his initials, G. E. Mortimer. The moderate climate drew many retirees to the city and the younger crowd, bored by teacups and trusses, dubbed Victoria 'the graveyard of the Pacific'.

Given up at birth by an unwed mother, I was adopted by Scottish immigrants whose disdain for frivolity suited the city well. At fifteen, I delivered newspapers every weekday afternoon to regular customers in downtown buildings. I was not a happy child. I hated my parents and I hated Victoria. One afternoon I took *The Daily Colonist* to an eccentric businessman. A bachelor millionaire, he rented a one-room office that smelled of the tinned soup and beans he heated on a dirty hotplate. He had no secretary; correspondence and yellowing newspapers were stacked on his desk and on the floor. He asked if I collected stamps, and when I shook my head, he said it was a hobby every boy should cultivate. He handed me a half-dozen envelopes. In the corridor, I looked at the millionaire's gift. A caribou struck a stately pose on a Newfoundland rock, a combine harvester swept up prairie grain. One of the foreign letters was Cuban. Giant palm trees decorated the stamp. I lingered in the corridor, looking at the return address. Judging something by its name is a mistake the young make more often than the old. Too young to understand this, I decided Havana was everything Victoria was not. Excitingly cosmopolitan; love and adventure amidst dancing palms and elegant white dwellings.

Decades later, approaching the city for the first time, I stopped at El Morro, the fifteenth-century fortress across the bay from Havana. From its elevated grounds, Havana didn't quite live up to my childhood expectations. There wasn't a palm tree in sight and the buildings weren't white, they were tinted yellow by the early morning sun. I had read the city's history. I knew pirates had attacked it and slaves had revolted in its streets, and that a district running west from the waterfront, Habana Vieja, contained so many examples of finely crafted colonial architecture that UNESCO had declared it a World Heritage Site. I also knew that although the Castro regime blamed ousted dictator Fulgencio Batista and his Mafia friends for creating the sex industry in the 1950s, Havana had a reputation for wantonness long before the *yanqui* criminals took root. Waterfront brothels prospered; so did back alley clubs staging live sex shows. In his 1939 book, *The Lawless Roads*, Graham Greene wrote: 'A Pennsylvanian with pouchy insomniac eyes warned me against Havana … "It's awful," he said, "the things they do. I've been to Paris, an' I can stand a lot, but these Cubans … the things they show you.'"

The extent of the skin trade in contemporary Havana is, by all accounts, insignificant compared to its pre-Revolution status, but following the reduction of Soviet economic aid in 1990, it did experience a surge in popularity. Nowadays, prostitutes cluster on the Malecón and frequent late-night discos, and groin-motivated travellers of both genders fly in from Mexico and Venezuela solely to utilise their services. Prostitution is the most visible sign of decadence in the city. Communism imposes an almost Calvinistic kind of discipline, morality and austerity in other areas. No advertising is approved for billboards and posters unless it preaches socialist gospel or promotes a state-involved business enterprise. The police harass known dissidents; foreign books and periodicals are banned; homosexuals are attacked in public, and in an effort to curb alcohol consumption, the government maintains steep prices for hard liquor. A few years ago, a Havana television station fostered orderly conduct by carrying a nightly message advising children that it was eight o'clock and time for them to go to bed.

There is, however, an element in the Cuban character that refuses to be totally controlled. Like some sort of deviant flower, Cubans blossom underground. They make their own booze, they pass outlawed American and Canadian magazines from person to person (so everyone can wistfully ogle the glossy ads for Reeboks and jeans and General Electric appliances), and they let their children stay up past eight o'clock. Published in England in 1994, self-exiled writer Guillermo Cabrera Infante's anti-Castro lament for his homeland, *Mea Cuba*, has been photocopied and secretly distributed amongst the city's intelligentsia. The offspring of a formerly rich family lock the doors, draw the curtains and assemble in the kitchen to indulge in a slice of forbidden fruit, playing a banned capitalist game. The original property titles on the wrinkled Monopoly board were changed by a now-dead family member to the names of bygone Batista-era Establishment hangouts. Players can imagine they're shopping for trendy American merchandise at El Encanto department store, eating baked Alaskas at El Carmelo café or dropping by the Montmartre, a nightclub modelled after the Moulin Rouge, to visually measure how high the cancan dancers kick.

Habaneros take small measures to alleviate government control over their personal lives, but there is a general feeling of despair regarding a long-entrenched policy they can do nothing about. Havana is crumbling. Once known as one of the world's loveliest capitals, the Paris of the western hemisphere, the city is an architectural stew – Baroque, Moorish, Art Nouveau – practically everything and anything that thrills the eye. The façades of private homes favour pinks and whites, yellows and greens, oranges and blues. But the deteriorating plaster, rusting wrought-iron and faded paint flaw the city's beauty, reminding you of a wedding cake left out in the rain. With few repair materials available and little money to purchase those that are, Habaneros pray the cash-strapped Castro government will somehow fund a massive renewal project. Some people don't pray, they rage. 'You can still enjoy it [Havana] before it collapses in shit,' a character says angrily in the Cuban film, *Strawberry and Chocolate*. 'Doesn't it pain them to see the city this way?'

Strolling through Centro Habana after lunch at the

Colonel's, I noticed men playing dominoes on a doorstep, an elderly woman with a bent spine carrying a caged chicken, a pretty teenage girl watching a street shoemaker fix her broken sandal. Laundry was draped over balconies and strung across courtyards. People lined up, empty containers in hand, outside a kerosene shop, and further on more people waited, ration books in hand, in front of a bakery. I came across a piece of nineteenth-century ornamental tile work on a building façade. Some of the tiles had fallen out and others were cracked. Looking at it, I thought of a local artist I had chatted with years earlier on a beach near Santiago de Cuba. I'd told him I'd been coming to the island since the 1980s, but that I'd only spent a single day in Havana.

'It's a beautiful place,' I said.

'Yes, it is,' was the artist's gloomy reply. 'A beautiful corpse.'

chapter three

A light rain was adding gloom to an already grey afternoon as I climbed out of the taxi at the Plaza de la Revolución. The miserable weather was actually a godsend. Miguel had warned me that on a clear summer afternoon the massive square, with its acres of bare concrete, was the hottest place in Havana. Even Cubans, who were born with heat-resistors in their systems, were known to collapse during marathon Castro speeches that drew half a million people to the plaza.

I hadn't come to hear El Comandante. The lure was the 60-foot statue behind the empty platform, the white marble figure of martyred poet José Martí. To understand contemporary Cuba, Miguel said, I had to understand Martí. I didn't anticipate receiving a whole lot of understanding from a statue, but for my Cuban odyssey, the monument was a natural starting point. Standing in the plaza, wet and impatient, I opened a notebook and scribbled on the first page: 'Martí's torso covered with a flowing Grecian robe. Everything white. Through the misty rain, he looms above the square like a pale, ominous ghost.'

Ascribing a ghostly connotation to the statue was a set-up for an old journalistic device, focusing a story by giving its topic symbolic significance. But, device or not, Martí did die in 1895, and like a spectre that won't rest in its grave, he did haunt Cuban society. His name popped up everywhere. At José Martí Airport, on José Martí Publishing

House books, on school and library façades, on parks and boulevards, peso notes and postage stamps. Ordinary citizens quoted his writings as if they were quoting from the Scriptures; small Martí busts adorned household shelves and office desks. The lionisation of the long-dead poet came from the heart, inspired by genuine admiration rather than a Hollywood-style merchandising campaign.

Physically, Martí was not baked from the clay national heroes generally come from. He wasn't the big, robust, charismatic leader personified by the likes of Fidel Castro. He was a slightly built, gentle-voiced soul with a high forehead, large eyes, a shrinking hairline and a chronic hernia problem. He lived frugally, dressing in frayed clothing and remaining faithful to his published oath, 'With the poor of the earth, I choose to cast my lot.' In portraits, he projected a solemn, intense image; here, you thought, was a man who after his first sexual experience probably proclaimed it was nice, but to be frank, he found it less exciting than literature and revolution.

His passion for both of these developed when he was a teenager. The son of a Havana civil servant, Martí fell under the spell of a teacher preaching the overthrow of the ruling Spanish regime. At sixteen, Martí wrote a sonnet for an underground newspaper that ended with the line, 'God be praised that at last Cuba breaks the hangman's noose that oppressed her and raises her head proud and free.'

He was arrested on sedition charges; the sonnet was read in court and he was sentenced to six years at the infamous Presidio Prison. In 1871, when he was eighteen, Martí was pardoned and deported to Spain. Defying the authorities, he wrote a book decrying the savage treatment he and other inmates suffered labouring on a penitentiary chain gang.

Martí studied law in Madrid and Zaragoza, and eventually settled in New York. He married a Cuban-born woman and paid the rent by teaching Spanish and writing newspaper articles. Neither domesticity nor his prodigious journalism output quelled his passion for independence from Spanish rule. During his fifteen-year stay in New York, he founded the Cuban Revolutionary Party and lectured widely on the evils of Spanish rule. In 1895 Martí chose action over words. He landed clandestinely in Oriente province and joined up with a guerrilla band. On 19 May he rode into a Spanish ambush at Dos Rios and was fatally shot. Decades later, the Cuban government published his collected works. They filled seventy-four volumes.

Learning of the mass affection for Martí that prevailed one hundred years after his death made me think about the situation in my own homeland. No historical figure in Canada was this revered. We may be grateful to Sir John A. Macdonald for patching the country into a confederation quilt, but we don't adore him, and our dead revolutionaries haven't done any better. The Americans have made praising their historical leaders an industry unto itself, and two of their grandest political heroes, Jefferson and Lincoln, are thoroughly ingrained in that nation's psyche. Still, I doubted either of them flung as broad a shadow over contemporary American society as Martí did over Cuba.

With thoughts like that filling my head, I wiped rain off the notebook cover and wrote inside, 'Martí all-pervasive. His presence so strong you almost feel he's alive.'

A 560-foot obelisk spiked the sullen air behind Martí's statue. There was an observation platform on top. A dented

Mercury pulled into the driveway in front of the monument and a young couple hopped out. The driver beeped his horn and sped away as the couple dashed to the tower entrance. Why would they go up there when the rain restricted the visibility? I guessed the answer. On damp days in crowded, costly Havana, free-admission public sites offered a degree of privacy that was hard to come by.

I turned and hurried across the square to the waiting taxi. It was a fairly new Datsun. The meter began running at $1, making the taxi off-limits to most Cubans. The driver stationed it outside a hotel favoured by foreign travellers, the $180 to $1,000 a night Nacional.

As the vehicle headed along Avenida Salvador Allende, I asked the driver if Martí had any children.

'We're all his children,' he replied.

'I mean actual sons and daughters.'

'Yes, a son and a daughter. His grandson's a famous actor in America. The name escapes me.'

'Andy García? He's Cuban.'

'Not him. Too young to be Martí's grandson.'

'Raúl Juliá?'

'He was Puerto Rican. Ah, I know. César Romero. Yes, César Romero. Martí's daughter, the illegitimate one, was his mother. So the story goes.' He adjusted the tiny Santa Barbara statue on the dashboard. 'You've heard the Martí song? It's very old.' Without prompting, he sang a few lines of a funereal melody. I wanted to write the lyrics down so he repeated them in a slow, deferential tone.

'Here's to the missing voice. Oh, the glorious voice. Of that Cuban nightingale. Of that brother and martyr. By the name of José Martí.' He stopped at a red light, turned his head and said, 'It goes on and on. Do your people have songs dedicated to your patriots?'

None, I said, that taxi drivers go around singing.

chapter four

Roberto came into the kitchen while I was sitting at the table drinking a coffee. He was hunting for a plastic bucket. When he found it under the sink, he turned my way with an amused expression that should have warned me something wasn't quite right.

'Want to go for a walk?'

'Sure. Your mother's in the bathroom. She might like to join us.'

'I think she's going back to work.' He stepped to the doorway and called to her. Yes, she shouted, she was due in half an hour at the institution where she was a dance teacher.

'It's just you and me,' Roberto said.

'Where are we going?'

'A house near the cigar maker's. I'm picking something up.'

Roberto was wiry and moustachioed. He wore a 'Free O.J.' T-shirt a cousin had sent to Cuba and he had a black-ink tattoo on his forearm, an angelic figure with his ex-girlfriend's name, Lupe, inscribed below it. I didn't care for Roberto. He was a smart-ass, forever bragging about how he had bettered somebody else. His most recent coup, according to him, was tricking 'a stupid tourist' into giving him a copy of *Penthouse* magazine; he cut the pictures out and sold them individually to his friends. Care for him or not, Roberto was a born and bred Habanero who recounted informative stories about life in his neighbourhood. Whenever he wanted to take me somewhere, I usually went.

Roberto fitted the lid on the bucket and we left the flat. I was soon swamped, as I had been before, by the knowledge that my negative view of Roberto wasn't shared by other people. He was adored. He sailed through the streets greeting men and women of all ages with handshakes, hugs and a standard Cuban gesture of affection, kissing cheeks. Roberto loved the snug familiarity of his home neighbourhood, but he dreamt of Florida, the enchanted city of Miami where, he said, big-bosomed blondes played beach volleyball and males his age, twenty-one edging twenty-two, owned motorscooters and denim jackets.

'When the weather's good, I hear the Florida stations on my radio,' he said. 'I hear the singers but I don't know what they look like. Is Annie Lennox black or white?'

'White.'

'Whitney Houston?'

'Black.'

'And Michael Jackson. Is he black or white?'

'Both.' I didn't get a chance to explain the circumstances of Jackson's birth colour and current skin condition. Roberto spied his uncle, Gustavo, who crossed the street and embraced Roberto. He was a stumpy, big-nosed man. Before shaking my hand, he slipped a partial plate from his pocket and slid it into his mouth. I resolved to wash my hand as quickly as possible.

'What have you got in the bucket, nephew?'

'Nothing,' Roberto said.

'You're walking the streets with an empty bucket,' Gustavo teased. 'Such a crazy kid. Carlota dropped you on your head lifting you out of your cradle.' Speaking to me, he said, 'La Ferminia's a rich place. Carlota must've been in paradise.'

'We couldn't find it. We drove around Miramar for an hour.'

'Juan never admits he doesn't know something. La Ferminia isn't in Miramar, it's in Flores. *Pendejo*. I wish Juan had gone north to Yuma the time he said he was going. And, you, Roberto, what were you doing on the Malecón with a *puta*? Such a goat. *Mucho macho*.'

Roberto placed a hand on Gustavo's shoulder and said irritably, 'Listen, uncle, I can't afford prostitutes and I wasn't doing anything. She was my classmate. I was sorry to see her there and I said so. Who saw me?'

'I haven't an answer. A friend told Nicolena and she told my wife. My taxi is calling. I hear it yelling my name. "Gustavo, come and drive me and earn some good tips today." *Hasta luego*.'

'*Hasta luego*, uncle.'

We resumed walking.

'We need a newspaper in this town. All we have is *Granma*. Two pages of government propaganda each week. If we had newspapers like you do, with tons of movie star gossip, ordinary people wouldn't be so fascinated by other ordinary people. Gossip's a sport here. Baseball for the mouth. Everyone's pitching and batting and your reputation's the ball. Hardly anybody has a telephone, yet you can talk to a girl for two minutes, miles from your house, and two days later your whole family knows.'

'That's pretty bad. When he was talking about Juan, your uncle said he wished he'd gone north to Yuma. What did he mean, "north to Yuma"?'

'Barrio language. It means sailing to Florida.'

'Yuma's in Arizona.'

'Who knows why they say Yuma. A Glenn Ford movie's been on television a hundred times. *3:10 to Yuma*. Maybe that's why. Or maybe we've got it all wrong. Maybe it should be "north to Ybor." Thousands of Cubans migrated to Ybor City in Florida before the First World War to work in the cigar factories.'

'I'm surprised American movies are shown here.'

'On television. Black and white pictures from before the Revolution. Sometimes pictures that are almost new are released in cinemas. *Runaway Bride, Shakespeare in Love*. The censors must have detected anti-American messages in them that I didn't detect.'

We entered a section of Centro Habana where if anyone knew Roberto, they didn't acknowledge it. Passing a haggard woman selling home-made biscuits in a doorway, I realised she was staring as though a Hallowe'en mask covered my face. I had donned my grungiest shirt and jeans to blend into the barrio landscape, but something about me flashed alien presence.

There weren't many buildings near Roberto's home that didn't plead for new paint and plaster, but houses in the section we entered were in worse condition. Some were vacant, likely condemned. Roberto led me into a derelict building. We proceeded to the rear. The window glass and the door were missing and the room smelled of mildew and rot. Roberto removed the bucket lid and laid it on the concrete floor.

'We'll set up camp here,' he said.

'Are you meeting somebody?'

'It won't be long.'

He stuck a piece of chewing-gum in his mouth and,

crouching inside the doorway, chewed slowly. I assumed he was waiting to meet someone who lived in the two-storey house across the lane. On the other side of a low brick wall, laundry dried in the yard; a roly-poly woman made a brief appearance in the kitchen. Roberto was transfixed.

'Newspapers,' he said. 'We had fifteen in this town. My grandmother read newspapers each and every day. *El País* was her favourite. It wrote the gossip – this guy was barred from the tennis club for cheating at bridge, that guy was arrested for stealing money from his boss. Perverts and crooks and rich guys divorcing their wives. She clipped stories from *El País* and glued them in a scrapbook. She's still got it, hidden somewhere. We were better off when people were gossiping about those things instead of each other.'

We waited twenty minutes. He said it wouldn't be much longer. Then another twenty minutes passed, and I was getting bored, anxious to return to my hotel and a cold Bucanero in the lounge.

'She's off her routine,' Roberto said. 'She should be out by now.'

'I'll only stay a few more minutes,' I said. 'I've got things to do.'

'Do you know the joke about Fidel's brother? Cubans despise the bastard. He's a cruel cockroach. One day, Raúl's visiting a dairy farm and he falls into a big hole filled with cow shit. It's in his mouth and throat and he's choking to death when the farmer yanks him out. "Please don't tell anyone I was stupid enough to fall in," Raúl begs the farmer. "I promise I won't," the farmer says, "if you promise not to tell anyone I saved your life."'

'Raúl's despised but Fidel isn't.'

'Right. We idolise Fidel. I can't understand why he doesn't hold an election. He'd win by a landslide. Fidel and José Martí – the courage of lions and the hearts of saints.' He unwrapped a fresh stick of chewing-gum.

I waited two or three minutes and then Roberto said happily, 'There she is. Here. Hold this.' He handed me the bucket and hurried into the lane. A scrawny white cat had leapt onto the brick wall.

Roberto stepped to the wall and grabbed the cat. It was a hot-tempered scrapper, twisting, clawing, and issuing furious noises.

'Quick! Bring me the bucket!'

I stayed put. I had stolen a lot of things when I was a youngster. I had ripped flowers from gardens on one street and sold them door to door on another. I had taken money from my father's wallet when he was drunk, and I had gone through the window of a neighbour's house to swipe a watch. But I had never stolen anything that had a brain.

With the frantic animal pressed against his chest, Roberto ran over and snatched the bucket. He shoved the cat inside and attached the lid. 'That was easy,' he said. 'Some scratches, but they'll heal.'

'I don't believe this,' I said.

'If you were forced to exist on a Cuban diet, you'd be taking cats too. I wanted you to see this. It's the "untouristy" Cuba you say you're looking for.' His face assumed the amused expression that was characteristic of him. 'You ought to be grateful we aren't eating tourists. The fat *pingas* soaked in suntan lotion fry real good.'

We went into the street. The cat had calmed down. It was crying softly.

'Does your mother know you steal cats?'

'How can she not know? She cooks our meals.'

'Jesus.'

'We've eaten strange food.'

'*Sopa de gallo*.'

'Yes. And pigeons and rodents. And boiled weeds for vitamins. No one's starving to death, but we're all desperate for some variety. A blind man went for a stroll on Calle 22. When he was standing on the corner, a thief cut the leash and stole his guide dog. The radio news said it was a purebred and valuable for breeding, but not a person in Havana believed that was the reason. We all knew the dog was a dinner table treat.'

I considered offering to buy the cat from him. Five bucks, American. But I didn't trust Roberto. He was too proud of his deceptions, his cleverness. He would pocket the cash, release the cat and steal it again when I wasn't around.

Roberto and I parted at an intersection. I had a busy summer ahead. Prearranged meetings, a bit of travelling and whatever else I happened to come across. I started walking in the direction of my hotel, intending to sip beer, think up interview questions and, if my guardian angel was on the job, forget all about the crying cat in the plastic container.

chapter five

Late at night, coming up to my room after a hike along the Malecón, I phoned Jessie in Toronto. I described a painting I had bought the previous day and would be bringing home. A declaration of feminine agony, it depicted a young Latin woman sprawled beneath the earth, her naked body wrapped in the roots of a flourishing tree. I wasn't in the habit of buying pictures in foreign lands, but the work, and its $400 price tag, was too compelling to resist.

Like many things in the country, Cuban art was undervalued. Manuel Mendive's almost primitive paintings, rife with supernatural symbols and figures, have garnered a fair amount of international praise. Yet a new wave of younger artists, like the Havana artist whose painting I bought, have gone largely unrecognised abroad, so their canvases sold for thousands of dollars below the North American market rates.

'I can't wait to see the painting,' Jessie said. 'Where are you going tomorrow?'

'Cristóbel Colón.'

'The cemetery? That ought to be fun. Well, maybe fun isn't the right word. You remember Miguel's story?'

'What story?'

'A 1930s coffee merchant was terrified of being buried alive. When he died his family installed a telephone in the mausoleum. You said you wondered who he'd call if he suddenly bolted to life, his wife or his mistress. Miguel said, "Neither. He'd ring the doctor who pronounced him dead and say he was racing over to beat him to death with the baseball bat he'd left him in his will.'"

'Yeah, I remember. And I remember thinking that must be a national custom I was unaware of. Willing your favourite bat to somebody.'

'Cubans are crazy about baseball but I doubt they're that crazy. Anyway, sweetheart, call me when you get back. I'd like to know if the phone's still in the tomb.'

It wasn't. The Castroites had apparently judged it to be a materialistic indulgence and ripped the line out around the same time they disconnected the air-conditioning units and removed the lifts from other mausoleums. Fortunately, the exteriors of all of the Cristóbel Colón mausoleums escaped post-Revolution correctness measures, more out of respect for the architecture than for their dead, once-wealthy occupants.

Walking through the graveyard in the summer heat, I remembered trying to persuade a publisher to commission a book on the great cemeteries of the world. I described Highgate's weedy paths and creepy, disintegrating chambers; I told him how enthralled I'd been by the stone horses, turtles and inscribed pillars dotting the forested Song Dynasty cemetery in Qufu, China. The publisher wasn't intrigued. Graveyards were associated with darkness and gloom, he said, unsettling reminders of the slippery hold we have on mortality. With most people on earth possessing similar views, Cristóbel Colón's special beauty, like the work of the younger generation of Cuban painters, was certain to remain largely unappreciated. Havana-born writer Alejo Carpentier, the father of magic realism in Latin American literature, voiced the opinion that the hundred-year-old cemetery on the edge of the Vedado district was a locale where *lo real maravilloso* existed in physical form.

Beyond the huge, ornate entrance gate, the most impressive cemetery portico in the Americas, lay a splendidly diverse assortment of funereal art. Statues of sobbing angels, placid saints and 30-foot Christs sculpted in white Carrara marble bore a dog's breakfast of influences: Renaissance, Grecian and Romanesque.

In death as in life, the rich dominated the scene. While the destitute were consigned to simple plots and the middle classes favoured headstones inscribed with sad messages, the elite built ostentatious mausoleums. Some were miniature replicas of their former mansions: bronze doors, crystal windows, stone pillars and domes. Other tombs were more bizarre in nature. A preference for the exotic spawned replicas of Arabian palaces, Egyptian pyramids, Gothic cathedrals and Grecian temples. The marble figure of a uniformed baseball player stood over a tomb filled with deceased athletes, umpires and managers, a ball's throw from the automobile club's mausoleum where a steering wheel was cast in bronze.

Steering wheels and pyramids … weeping angels and towering Christs … lifts and air conditioning …

I toured the graveyard, concurring with Carpentier's assessment that Cristóbel Colón was the material embodiment of magic realism. I continued to agree as I headed towards the portico and busy Calzade Zapata. But another word came to me that was, I reasoned, an equally suitable description for the burial place. The word was kitsch.

With an imaginative flourish, the American art critic

Clement Greenberg dubbed kitsch 'vulgaris triumphus'. That dismissive summation was his smart-tongued response to the sudden spread of the art form in America in the 1940s, roughly three decades after it gained huge popularity in Germany. The US version far out-vulgared the German. By the 1960s, millions of American home-owners possessed such items as Mona Lisa shower curtains, hymn-playing musical teapots and Donald Duck lawn ornaments. Derived from the German word *verkitschen* ('to make cheap'), kitsch's broad range included painting, sculpture, architecture and decor that, regardless of the cost, looked tacky, sentimental or excessively ornamental. Cristóbel Colón cemetery was a fine example of all of those things on a grand scale. So was another Havana landmark: the Tropicana.

Opened in 1939, the cavernous nightclub introduced the Cuban public to the brand of glittery, upbeat floor shows that were to become a Las Vegas staple. The Tropicana was expected to be a prime target of anti-capitalist elimination squads, perishing along with the brothels, casinos and live sex shows that existed during the Batista years. The Castroites astonished and pleased the populace by excluding the Tropicana from their death list so that the common folk who couldn't afford to go there in the old days would finally be accorded the pleasure. That was the official reason. No one suggested otherwise, yet I had a feeling that the actual reason involved a bunch of lard-bellied, middle-aged Party mandarins who desired a nocturnal refuge where they could soak their personal disappointments and anxieties in five-year-old rum while staring in an unfatherly manner at leggy young dancers.

On the night I went to the Tropicana, every table was full, which wasn't surprising. The club had retained its ability to mount one of the world's splashiest stage shows. Beyond fountains and statues of nude females at the entrance, the Cubans and foreigners gathered in the open-air setting whistled, hooted and clapped at dancers swinging their hips to Latin rhythms.

The gaudy costumes were a breath-stealing example of what the phrase 'excessively ornamental' meant. There were beads, baubles and sequins, ruffles and fringes, peacock tails and feathered boas. As the dancers wove their body magic, platoons of slender women floated about in the background wearing high-heeled shoes and Carmen Miranda-like headdresses containing imitation palm trees, sunflowers and authentic chandeliers and clocks.

Prior to the 1960s, Nat King Cole, Josephine Baker and Cab Calloway performed at the Tropicana: the night I was there the celebrity guest was a Cuban baritone whose repertoire of sentimental love songs added a vocal component to the atmosphere of premium-grade kitsch.

The inspiration, or blame, for importing 'vulgaris triumphus' to the island can be attributed to the sugar barons. The prospect of being buried at a kitsch haven like Cristóbel Colón obviously wasn't enough for them, for they made the 'art' form part of their daily lives. In the parlours of the rich and tasteless, busts of Beethoven and Mozart faced overly elaborate mantle clocks, stuffed owls under glass, glazed figurines, bronze Venus and Adonis statues, button-embedded chesterfields, framed Niagara Falls postcards, and paintings of cherished hunting dogs and children looking so adorable house guests must have hated them.

The ruling classes' affection for objects of limited artistic merit gradually spread to the cultural mainstream. Kitsch's popularity eventually expired in its German birthplace, but it never went out of style in Cuba. It was too colourful, too much fun to drop, like a disreputable old friend whose flashy charm swayed you to accept his sins. In Havana today, you encounter touches of kitsch in middle-income households – plaster frogs, garish lamp shades, sunset-on-the-beach pictures encased by seashell frames. On a Parque Central pathway, I passed a woman whose appearance was a mute tribute to kitsch; her striped cap was covered in tiny, round spangles, her fingernails were painted scarlet, she wore hoop earrings, a fake-snakeskin belt dotted with rhinestones, jungle-patterned shorts and pink running shoes.

Canadian writer Jane Suderman recalled meeting a Cuban photographer in 1992 whose pictures of teenage girls were very kitschy. 'Tony specialises in *trompe l'œil*,' she wrote in a *Globe and Mail* travel article. 'He showed me a collection of photographs of smiling fifteen-year-olds appearing to pose in the mouth of a Havana Club rum bottle, or at the top of the Havana Libre Hotel, or in a cocktail glass, swimming in a daiquiri.'

By tradition, Communism casts a suspicious eye on nonconformity. It was, after all, nonconformists like Lenin, Mao and Castro who upset the apple-carts in their homelands. Wary of appearing to march to a different drummer, countless people conceal their opinions and dress conservatively in public, even in their leisure hours. At home, behind closed doors, the story changes. Their compulsion to assert themselves as distinct individuals has helped keep the kitsch flame alive and blazing.

In the Vedado, a central Havana enclave where the moneyed elite used to inhabit posh houses and apartment suites, a lawyer named Juan Rafael Roca met me in the marbled lobby of a baroque-style building. He was a study in severity: heavy-framed glasses, black hair flawlessly parted and slicked down, a pinched mouth and cool eyes. Climbing the stairs to his fourth-floor flat, he said the lift had stopped functioning several months ago. The part the repairman required was unavailable on the island and had been ordered from a company in Madrid.

'People are kinder in hard times,' he said. 'You'd think it would be the opposite, but it isn't. In this building, an elderly lady on the third floor broke her leg and couldn't use the stairs. The elevator broke and a man on the bottom floor, a stranger, traded apartments with her. They are sleeping in each other's beds and cooking on each other's stoves until the elevator's fixed, which could be months and months.'

Juan's bubbly wife greeted us at the door. She was going to Cuatro Caminos, a free-enterprise farmers' market the state sanctioned in the wake of a 1990 Havana food riot. The prices were steep ($1.50 for a pound of rice, $1 for two lemons) but her gratitude over having the market and its three hundred vendors convinced her not to gripe about the costs.

When she was gone, Juan took me into the living room and showed me his pigs. There were legions of them. Ceramic pigs, alabaster pigs, pigs cut from plywood, pigs banged out of plastic moulds. I gazed at a piggy ashtray, a piggy lighter, an ornamental piggy outhouse, piggy drinking glasses and piggy napkin holders. Cutey-cute and tacky linked arms and marched around the room.

'Carlos, Magaly and I were students together,' Juan said, leading me to a snapshot of a real-life pig lying in a shower stall. 'This is Anibal. She sleeps in the stall. Carlos and Magaly are in one of those odious apartment blocks the

Russians constructed. They take Anibal walking on a lead. She's a very special pet, considering the dollars she would bring on the black market.'

The plywood outhouse with a grinning pig filling the seat had an English inscription, 'Who Sez We Ain't Clean?' Juan's brother got the trinket in Toronto; he worked for Cubana Airlines and had an eye open for piggy merchandise on foreign trips.

'No, I've never owned a real pig,' Juan said. 'An American boy gave me a Porky Pig comic book when I was a child and I absolutely adored it. Why do I collect these things? They amuse me. That's the best answer I can think of.'

Did his wife love the pigs?

'Love, no. Accept, yes. I swore that when we had the money, she could collect music boxes. How about you? Are my pigs appealing?'

'They're cute. Really cute.'

'In the fifties nodding-head toys were in fashion, particularly dogs sitting on car dashboards. I saw a nodding-head pig when I was an adolescent, and I'd be overjoyed to own it now. Pigs are intelligent and affectionate. Clean. Whoever invented the insult, "You filthy pig", did them a disservice.'

My final question was delicately broached. He didn't understand what I meant when I said kitsch, and unable to find a translation in my pocket dictionary, I stopped myself from saying 'bad taste' in case he was offended. So I inquired whether he knew anyone whose decorative choices leaned towards unique objects, maybe knick-knacks, maybe charcoal sketches of famous singers, stuff you wouldn't normally find in a fancy art gallery.

'There's a client of mine,' he replied slowly. 'I'm not sure you'd care to be with him.'

'What's the problem?'

'He's – how should I say it? – he's a *mariposa.*'

Cubans had at least four definitions for that word. Two were officially accepted parts of the language, 'butterfly' and 'wing nut', and the other two, 'fashion model' and 'homosexual', were street slang. From the way the lawyer referred to him, as if he was warning me against inhaling a repugnant odour, I had no doubt Jorge Figarola Cruz was gay.

chapter six

Jorge Figarola Cruz lived on La Rampa, not far from Juan's home. His flat was on the eighteenth floor of a modern apartment block and mercifully, the lift was working. The black and white comedy-tragedy masks and the yellow, three-foot-long cotton alligator in Jorge's vestibule were a harbinger. Beyond them, in the jumbled living room, nestled an accumulation of mismatched articles that established a zany, refinement-scorning mood. A big-eyed papier mâché cat observed a Mexican bull fight poster. A doll wrapped in a wedding gown was positioned in a corner of a brocade-upholstered couch.

'Señor Roca said you're writing a story about unusual decor,' Jorge said. 'What's unusual to you is normal to me. Is this unusual? Surely there are thousands of similar rooms in your country.'

'No, I don't think there are. What do you do for a living?'

'I'd rather not say. And please don't print my real name.' He laughed and said, 'If you're describing me, say I'm heart-breakingly handsome and exceptionally intelligent. Say my humorous tongue had you rolling on the floor. Nobody will recognise Jorge Figarola Cruz from that description.'

I settled on a rattan chair. Jorge made tea in the alcove kitchen, Earl Grey, which he said was a gift from a British businessman. He moved gracefully, a silver-haired, lean-bodied man in his late fifties. His voice was arresting: a measured, confident baritone. Was he an actor? A radio announcer? I regretted not asking Juan what Jorge's profession was.

I surveyed the clutter. There was a lacquered toy piano, a ceramic unicorn, a Victorian umbrella stand, a brown Bakelite radio, a mermaid plaque and a brass monkey. Plastic duelling pistols and a bevelled glass mirror, framed in dark oak, hung on the walls. I thought of a second-hand shop I knew in Toronto, a cubbyhole with hundreds of objects piled on both sides of the narrow aisle where it took a slow, hard perusal to spy a desirable antique.

'You must've had difficulty acquiring some of these items,' I said as Jorge poured tea into china cups.

'Not really. Sometimes the small expensive things were hidden under floors. Many Cubans thought the Revolution was doomed and the *yanquis* were coming back soon.' He emitted a short laugh. 'Can you imagine the things they've been walking on since 1959? Eisenhower inaugural plates. America-Cuba Friendship Society buttons.'

I chuckled and said, 'Your couch looks Edwardian.'

'Yes, the design's Edwardian but who can say if it's a reproduction? Do you know of the Frenchman, Rene Lalique? I have something. It may be genuine, and it may not.'

He fetched a circular powder box from the bedroom. It was Art Nouveau and crafted out of pale green frosted glass. Winged nymphs, bare-bosomed and long-haired, graced the lid. Was it an authentic Lalique? Like Jorge, I wasn't qualified to tell.

'Did somebody hide this under their floor?'

'No, it belonged to a department store owner. The government seized his house and my father was among the officials assigned to list the contents. The furnishings were a mixture of excellent reproductions and genuine European antiques. The antiques were trucked to museums. My father was infatuated with this box. Love at first sight. He shoved it in his pocket. But he always felt guilty. So guilty that a year or two later he hunted for the department store owner. The man and his wife were in Miami, but their daughter was here. My father turned the box over to her. She was so awed by his act that she bequeathed it to him. Last summer my father died and the box was passed on to me.'

'Someone in Havana should be able to appraise it.'

'It doesn't really matter. Its sentimental value is more important than its dollar value, whatever that may be. I'll never sell it.'

Between sips of tea, I told him I believed homes like his were citadels of individualism in a conformist landscape.

Jorge nodded. 'If the bloodless, boring hard-core fanatics were in control our homes would be decorated exclusively with Karl Marx icons and patriotic placards. Thank goodness, the common-sense Communists are in the majority and we haven't been completely stripped of our private identities. Our homes are truly our castles. In many instances, the urge to assert oneself as a distinct individual can be dangerous. It can be judged rebellious. A finger in the eye. *Playboy* magazine is banned. A friend of mine papered his bathroom wall with Playmates. Should the Committee for the Defence of the Revolution get wind of it, he'll be reported. The police will invade his apartment in the dead of night and tear down the anti-Communist breasts. A judge will reprimand my friend for anti-revolutionary activity and impose a stiff fine. Interior design as a defiant gesture. Interior decor as a protest against Marxist solemnity. Now there's a topic for a novel.'

'Who'd publish it? Nobody in Cuba.'

'For certain. Censorship and persecution have driven our best writers abroad. Infante is in England, Reinaldo Arenas died in New York City. Have you read any Cuban writers?'

Carpentier, I said, and Desnoes, Cabrera Infante and Lezama. The fourth name excited Jorge. Lezama was, he enthused, the Cuban author he admired the most, both as a novelist and as a person. That was understandable. José Lezama Lima was a darling of the Castro government until 1966. His poems were declared works of genius and he was appointed vice-president of the Cuban Artists' and Writers' Union. Then he wrote *Paradiso*, a novel dealing with the emotional struggles of a turn-of-the-century homosexual. There were no thrashing-body bedroom scenes, but in a lengthy passage the hero's erudite friend spoke of homosexuality amongst the ancient Greeks and feudal Japanese warriors and, quoting sexologist Havelock Ellis, he stated that 75 per cent of upper-crust British males had engaged in homosexual acts. By publishing *Paradiso*, Lezama, the shining star, transformed himself into a black hole. The novel was banished from bookshops and libraries, and Lezama himself was vilified and shunned by his intellectual colleagues. He died in Havana in 1976.

'So you've read *Paradiso*?' Jorge asked. 'I assume it impressed you. It's a masterpiece.'

'To be honest, it put me to sleep.'

'You're joking!'

'Too many dense paragraphs I had to read twice to fathom. Not much of a plot either, and some awfully long segments about preparing and eating meals.'

'Food was an obsession of Lezama's. He was an obese fellow who was known to drop by a bakery and consume two dozen cookies. If you hated the writing, you must admire the writer. Producing *Paradiso* was a brave deed. He frequented male bordellos and he was lucky not to be jailed. Reinaldo Arenas was gay, you know. He spent a year in a Morro dungeon for seducing a minor, even though the fellow he seduced was in his twenties. Arenas yearned to go to America, and when he finally went, it was a free trip – the Mariel boatlift, when Castro relaxed the immigration laws.'

'I'm unfamiliar with Arenas' writing. Was he a novelist?'

'Novels and poetry. His best novel, *Farewell to the City*, was translated into English. Your Toronto library must have a copy. He wrote the novel in Havana and the police searched his home and confiscated the manuscript. Twice, they did that; confiscated the manuscript and locked it away in a filing cabinet in a police basement. Arenas rewrote *Farewell to the City* without notes, strictly from memory. There are lines I've never forgotten. "Homosexuals collect anxieties and polished stones on beaches under surveillance. Homosexuals with two thousand years of persecution, imbued with the air of a hawk in flames."'

The authorities felt free to harass homosexuals without fear of an upper-level backlash. The nation's most renowned gay-hater was, after all, Fidel Castro. At a 1979 May Day rally in the Plaza de la Revolución, assailing the 'lumpen' and 'delinquent' members of society, he singled out 'limp-wristed, shameless creatures' for special censure. Thinking of Castro's well-known views, I gathered the official attitude hadn't changed. I was mistaken.

'The situation has improved,' Jorge said. 'Homosexuals

aren't rounded up in mass raids and confined in prison camps like they were in the sixties. Being gay wasn't illegal, but the government invoked an ancient law that covered a multitude of crimes, the Improper Conduct Act, to support its crackdown. Thousands of gays were sent to rehabilitation camps in the province of Camagüey. By day, they listened to lectures praising women and pretended to leer at photographs of splendid female specimens. At night, they loved each other. Did you see *Strawberry and Chocolate*? An openly gay character forms a close friendship with a heterosexual man. The government financed the movie and released it worldwide. That was a breakthrough for Cuban gays. Up there on the big screen was government-approved acknowledgement that gays can be warm, sympathetic human beings and not depraved animals deserving to be locked up in prison camps.'

Although the authorities no longer vigorously track down and detain homosexuals, anti-gay incidents do occur. Police roughed up several participants at Havana's first Gay Pride celebration in 1994, and male or female homosexuals holding hands in public risk having ordinary citizens curse, spit at or physically assault them. In recent years, 'ten peso' parties have emerged as an immensely popular facet of gay culture. For a ten-peso fee, a group of homosexuals rent a house for a BYO gathering.

'The "ten peso" parties are fairly safe,' Jorge said. 'If they're raided, it's usually because a neighbour complains that the noise is driving them nuts. In this society, blatantly obvious gays, the flamboyant types, are in danger of offending somebody's macho sensitivities and being reported and jailed, in spite of the more tolerant environment. The best policy is to avoid being noticed. The

Chinese say it beautifully. "The nail that rises up is hammered down." Ah, your cup's empty. You care for more tea?'

I studied the clutter. A Pérez Prado album leaned against a table leg. Plaster swans peered at a Harlequin figurine; a cotton shark had a fish bowl to itself. Without actually verbalising it, Jorge had informed me he was gay, and in a society obeying the edicts of cocky, pistol-wearing men in battle fatigues, the embodiment of faggot-despising masculinity, he walked on eggshells. His predicament cast his surroundings in a new perspective. Immersing himself in kitsch wasn't simply a device to retain individuality; it was an escapist necessity.

I also revised my interpretation of the painting I'd purchased. Because a woman created it, I had labelled it feminine angst. The subterranean victim, I now theorised, represented the artist and Jorge Figarola Cruz and millions of Cubans, straight and gay, who seldom left home before burying unorthodox attitudes and behaviour in deep, dark places.

chapter seven

Havana was wrapped in the unloving arms of a mid-summer heatwave. Thirty-four degrees in the afternoon sun and the humidity was aggravating every living thing. Down on the Malecón a pair of short-skirted prostitutes, endeavouring to entice early-bird clients before nightfall and normal business hours, had stationed themselves in front of the seawall. Shunning their suggestive glances, I went to a spot a few feet away and gazed towards Florida, ninety miles to the north. The prostitutes began to argue.

'You're ugly. Be someplace else.'

'Me ugly? That's a joke, Lucia. Your teeth are crooked and the rest of you is crooked too.'

'It's your face men can't stand. How long we been here? Hours. Go someplace, Juanita. I can't make no money near you.'

'OK, I'll go. You're evil, Lucia. The devil worships you.'

There was rancour in their voices, yet both Lucia and Juanita spoke softly, just above a whisper. Their hateful words floated like black balloons through sultry air heavily scented with ocean salt and lurid perfume. I had come to the waterfront in search of a *jinetera* (jockey, Cuban slang for prostitute), to interview. Listening to the conversation between Lucia and Juanita, I dismissed them as potential subjects because they were too common, too unintelligent. I was seeking a specific creature, a prostitute with a Ph.D.

'Times are tough,' a Canadian teaching in Cuba had enlightened me. 'Girls come out of the University of Havana with Ph.D.s in their hands, and within months, they're working the streets.' An article published in GQ lent credence to his statement. Under the headline 'Ten Holidays You Wouldn't Want To Take Your Girlfriend On', an anonymous writer claimed Cuban prostitutes were 'tall, glossy, beautiful' and the 'best-educated whores in the world.'

They weren't all tall, glossy and beautiful – although I had never seen a truly unattractive Cuban prostitute – but I was willing to believe that because university education was free, many women gained degrees or completed post-graduate studies before taking to the streets.

As Juanita strutted away, I started walking in the opposite direction. Prostitution was illegal, and every now and then the police scooped the practitioners off the boulevard, sometimes jailing them, sometimes demanding bribes for not jailing them. Two prostitutes were up ahead. Spotting a police car, they turned their backs to the road and feigned fascination with a fishing line an elderly man was dangling over the wall. The police car crept by. When it was gone, the women swung around. Both were young, slim and pretty. The shorter of the two was wearing jeans and a striped halter-neck top, her companion bell-bottoms and a LaCoste polo shirt. Assessing their educational level by listening to their dialogue was, I decided, really moronic. Lucia and Juanita could've been academic superstars who, embracing whoredom, adopted street-life speech patterns.

'Hello,' I said, walking up to them. 'I'm a writer from Canada. I was wondering if either of you have a university degree.'

The women traded incredulous glances. Then they were overcome by giggling fits.

'I'm sorry we're laughing,' the bell-bottomed *jinetera* said. 'Men ask weird questions. This is one of the weirdest.'

'We can't get degrees for what we do,' the other woman said. 'It isn't taught in school.'

When the giggling trailed off, I explained that I was writing about prostitution and wanted a different slant. Neither of them had encountered a Ph.D. holder, but the woman in bell-bottoms said she knew a *puta* who had graduated from the University of Havana with a biological science degree. 'Her name's Delisa. She's extra smart.'

'Where can I find her?'

'I'll ask her to meet you. Is tomorrow night OK? Bring a small present. I'm Elena. I'll be with her and you can bring me a small present too.'

Small presents were no problem. I bought shampoo in the hotel giftshop. Because Cubans' near-obsessive desire for cleanliness was severely hampered by the American embargo, sexual favours were often paid for with a bar of soap or a bottle of shampoo. When soap and shampoo wouldn't do, and Cokes and chocolate bars didn't excite the *jineteras*, the cash rate was between $3 and $100, depending upon the seller's estimation of her own self-worth.

I met Elena the following night on Calle Obispo, opposite the Hotel Ambos Mundos where a room Ernest Hemingway had rented was reverently kept unoccupied. She was dressed in the same shirt and bell-bottoms and she was alone. Delisa was unable to travel across the city, but if I'd pay the taxi fare, Elena would escort me to her. I gave Elena the shampoo. She seemed to be in a sullen mood;

she stared out of the taxi window. On the Malecón I had had the impression she was roughly eighteen years old. Studying her heart-shaped face now, it occurred to me that I may have been wrong. Girls as young as twelve were reportedly working in the sex industry: Elena wasn't twelve, I was positive of that, but she might not be far past it.

'Elena, I'm curious. How old are you?'

'Who cares?' she shrugged. 'It isn't important.'

'You're right, it isn't important.'

'You want me to be twenty, I'll be twenty. You want me to be fifteen, I'll be fifteen. Whatever pleases you.'

'It isn't what I want. It's what you really are.'

'Eighteen. That's my real age. Eighteen.'

The taxi conveyed us to a large house in Miramar. The brass plaque next to the door read 'El Palacio de la Moda'. A fashion house on this impoverished island? Impossible. It had to be a cover for an elegant brothel.

We left the taxi.

'You don't seem very content,' I ventured.

'I'm not.'

'Did someone upset you?'

'I upset myself. A man met me on the Malecón and took me to dinner at the Riviera. I slept with him. I hate myself for it. Delisa's right. I shouldn't sleep with a man because he takes me to a restaurant. I promised her I wouldn't do it anymore, but I was really hungry. And now I regret it. Delisa would never sell herself that cheaply. You'd be impressed by the beautiful things she owns. Presents from lovers. Jewellery and clothes. Delisa's waiting. Go inside. I'll stay here. The doorman won't let me in.'

'What does she look like?'

'I've described you. She'll come to your table.'

El Palacio was the fashion centre it purported to be. Attired in Cuban-made leisurewear, females with more bone than flesh walked along a catwalk while Cream performed 'Sunshine of Your Love'. Some of the thirty-odd people in the room were writing notes. International buyers, the waiter said, and scouts from European modelling agencies. I drank a Cuba Libre. The show ended and a female MC announced that a bathing suit presentation was scheduled for the following evening. Cream was replaced by salsa music. Delisa failed to appear. I worried that I was the victim of a shampoo scam and Elena and her Malecón friend would be giggling themselves into convulsions.

Delisa finally approached my table. She was tall and graceful, a bottle-blonde in her mid or late twenties. She had changed the beach outfits she'd worn in the show for a cream-coloured linen suit.

'We aren't allowed to sit with customers,' she said. 'I received special permission. I claimed you were a fashion writer.'

Delisa talked freely and unashamedly. Her father was a trucker, her mother a shop assistant and, yes, she had earned a biological science degree at the University of Havana. It was a scarcely known fact that Cuba was a world leader in biotechnical research. A huge Havana laboratory produced, among other items, vaccines used to treat hepatitis B and the cancer-fighting drug, Interferon. Delisa was a member of the research staff, and though she liked her job, she was sick of the $10-a-month wages. One day, a male co-worker pointed out a nicely dressed office manager at the bus stop and sneeringly remarked that she was a part-time prostitute. The co-worker unwittingly planted a seed.

'The woman looked well fed and content. I was miserable.

I was practically starving myself to save up enough pesos to buy a good dress in four months' time. A married guy I worked with was pestering me to go to Parque Lenin. A picnic, the two of us. He would come up to me in the lab and sing the Lecuona song, '*Siempre en Mi Corazón*' [Always in My Heart] under his breath. I said to him, "Get me the dress I'm saving for and I'll wear it on our picnic." He got it but I didn't wear it. Too precious for a picnic. Anyway, every time I slept with him, I made him pay. There were rumours at the lab and my boss hinted I was going to be in trouble. I resigned and went to modelling classes. And that's when I started meeting foreign men.'

Three nights a week, Delisa solicited tourists at discos. If they couldn't go to their hotel rooms because their wives were there, she took them to the flat she shared with her mother and sister. She was fatigued, but she managed to fool the clients into believing she was having a rapturous time. She had terminated the disco-prowling upon signing on at the fashion centre.

'Modelling's easy, but the pay stinks. Ten dollars a month, the identical salary I got at the laboratory. But I have boyfriends now, Mexicans, Canadians and Germans. Businessmen and diplomats, men with money to spend.'

'Where do you meet them?'

'Here. El Palacio.'

'I thought consorting with customers was forbidden.'

'We can't sit. We can stand and talk. Fashion trade people come to El Palacio, but most of our clients are tourists. Lonely men, forty and up. That guy over there, that's Colin. He's British. Mária, his girlfriend, she's a model. He's buying a house in Pinar del Río.'

'I thought it was illegal for non-Cubans to own property.'

'It was. The National Assembly changed the law. Colin's paying twenty thousand dollars. The government researched the title and assured him the house had been owned by a local family for generations. It has never belonged to a Florida Cuban who could try to reclaim it someday. Mária's family will live in it after they marry and move to London.'

Colin was slumping at a ringside table, draining a pina colada. He was ruddy-cheeked, sandy-haired, flabby-bellied and fiftyish. He had been married twice, Delisa said, and he had dazzled Mária by showing her snapshots of his car and stereo equipment.

'Mária says he's a perfect catch,' Delisa said. 'He plays darts and he takes his mother for a car ride on Sunday. He's known Mária six months and he's slept with her four times. I say good luck to her. I'm not surprised two women divorced him. The lead in his pencil doesn't write.'

'Are all the models *jineteras*?'

'It depends on your definition of a *jinetera*. A few of the girls come right out and say, "Give me cash or keep your pants on." There are forty models here, and I'd say a third of them go to bed with foreigners, hoping they'll marry them. And sometimes they do get married. I call that prostitution, marrying for money.'

Colin emptied his glass and signalled the waiter for a refill.

'That man's brain-damaged,' Delisa scowled. 'He knows ten words of Spanish and he can't get them right. *Piña colada*. He mispronounced it every night, and Mária finally said, "Colin, please, some girls in this place are prostitutes but the drinks here don't have sex names. It's *piña colada*, OK? *Piña colada* – not penis colada."'

Delisa had to return to work. She escorted me to the front door.

'Do your boyfriends treat you differently because you're a bright lady and you've been to university?'

'I don't let them know. Men prefer girls less intelligent than themselves. A relationship can't work unless the man feels superior, and he won't feel superior if he knows you're as intelligent, or more intelligent, than he is.'

Was it possible for me to interview her parents?

'My parents? They've been apart for years. My father's in Santa Clara and we don't have his address. I'm certain my mother won't mind seeing you. She'd love a small gift. Elena will set up a meeting.'

'She knows your mother?'

'Of course. Elena's my sister.'

chapter eight

Teresa's flat was an oven. A power cut stilled the fan and without a breeze in the air, the open windows did little to ease the humidity. Sweat stuck to Teresa's forehead and darkened the armpits of her faded cotton dress. She accepted my presents gratefully. The perfume went onto a living room shelf beside other bottles of imported fragrance, displayed in their boxes like hard-won trophies. The chocolate bars were stored in the venerable refrigerator.

The decor was predominantly vintage Vatican. Plaster statues of the Virgin Mary and various saints, pictures of the Last Supper and of Christ blessing children, a tiny cross above each doorway. How did Teresa's religious convictions accommodate the fact that both of her daughters were prostitutes and at least one of them, Delisa, used to bring her clients home? Perhaps, I thought, her attitude was similar to that of a Mafia hitman. Killing people had no bearing on whether or not you were a good Catholic; business and religion were separate practices.

'Communism and Christianity are natural-born enemies,' I commented. 'The cobra and the mongoose.'

'The Church is the stronger of the two,' she said. 'When it suffers, it tightens its grip and survives. When Communism suffers, like in Russia, it loses its grip and collapses.'

'The Catholic Church nearly collapsed in Cuba.'

'With respect, señor, that is false propaganda. There are millions of Catholics here. When the Communists started persecuting them, Catholics didn't renounce their faith, they hid it. Religious holidays are banned, and that includes Christmas. Millions of people can be handcuffed, but they can't be stopped altogether. We celebrate religious holidays in our homes. At Christmas, we pin paper stars and drawings of the holy manger to our walls. Now the government's more friendly to us. No, wait – friendly isn't correct. Tolerant. The government's more *tolerant* of us. True Catholics and hard-core Communists will never be bosom buddies, but we can learn to live together.'

The perfume packages weren't the only trophies in the room. The new couch was covered with a loose-fitting plastic sheet, and Elena had warned me that the wrapped sweets in the coffee-table dish were not to be eaten, they were a symbol of affluence. The plastic rustled when I sat on it.

Perched on an aluminium patio chair, Teresa was attentive and polite. She was a striking woman, the undeniable source of her daughters' beauty, but her hips were exceptionally broad and her bosom drooped. 'There is an exquisite moment between thirty and thirty-five when Cuban women suddenly pass from maturity to rottenness,' says the decadent hero of the Tomás Gutiérrez Alea film, *Memories of Underdevelopment*. 'They are fruits that rot at an amazing speed.'

'When Elena phoned me this morning, she said you weren't opposed to her and Delisa becoming prostitutes.'

'I wasn't against Elena, señor. She was a poor student and a sweet face was the best card in her deck. Delisa was different. A brilliant student, top of her class. I got a pain in my heart when she went into prostitution. A pain in my heart. But it was my fault, not hers. Mother lions teach their babies how to hunt. When Delisa was a child and I needed something, I got money doing what she's doing. The way she behaved in the mornings, glaring at the men, I thought she despised prostitution and would never do it. I was wrong, señor. I was wrong.'

Teresa and her husband were from Oriente, the eastern province that produced both Fulgencio Batista and Fidel Castro. Her mother was a middle-class merchant's wife who, suddenly deserted by her bankrupt husband, went to work at a Santiago whorehouse. Teresa's prostitution began at fourteen, halted when she married, and resumed sporadically after her husband ran off to Santa Clara with a younger woman. Religion was Teresa's life-saver; religion spared her from the depression and alcoholism that befell prostitutes when age and a world-weary demeanour devalued the product they were marketing.

'I had a turning point when I was young,' Teresa said. 'My mother was forcing me to sleep with a regular of hers, a fat old farmer with scaly skin and red blotches on his face. A pig in man's clothing. I went to confession and told the priest the things the farmer did to me. When I came out of the box, the priest grabbed my arm. He dragged me to the back of the church and made me masturbate him. Then he wept and accused himself of evil acts. He was such a tortured soul that I stayed a long time, comforting him. On that day, it dawned on me that prostitution wasn't completely bad. *Putas* have an important role in the world. They give men a little pleasure, a little happiness.'

'I'm surprised the fact that he was a priest didn't sour you on the Catholic Church.'

'One impure priest doesn't mean the Church itself is impure. Just as my sins don't mean I'm impure and beyond salvation. The Lord's mansion has many rooms, señor, and I'm sure He'll have space for me.' She climbed to her feet. 'This is where I pray.'

The burnt-down candles and the Virgin Mary statue were on a wooden stand in Teresa's bedroom. She prayed three times a day, more if she was greatly troubled. The green and yellow bedcover was, she said, a gift from Delisa. The girls contributed the lamp, the Britney Spears' calendar and the Chinese fan over the bed. A closet contained unopened cartons of German cigarettes (none of the three women smoked), a tartan bathrobe, blouses and sweaters, a portable typewriter, a stapler, a touch-tone telephone and cardboard boxes filled with unspecified prostitute-loot. She was keeping the merchandise in pristine condition until she was older and presumably infirm and was forced to sell it.

'I pray Delisa will go back to the laboratory,' Teresa said. 'She behaves as though prostitution is great fun. I know it isn't. I met foul men in my day. I've noticed bruises on her arms, the black eye under the make-up. Sex gives men pleasure, señor, but it doesn't make them nicer people.'

Several days after I visited Teresa's flat, Delisa phoned me at the hotel. Her mother had enjoyed our meeting and Elena sent me her good wishes.

'How old is your sister?' I inquired.

'Elena? She's sixteen. Do you want her for a girlfriend?'

'No. I just suffer from incurable curiosity.'

'How else do you suffer? Are you lonely? I telephoned to see if you'd like me to drop by your hotel.'

There was no mistaking her message. I perked up, an

eager recruit. Delisa was the kind of tall, glossy beauty *GQ* raved about. As quickly as it gleamed, temptation blackened. My wife was my closest friend; I had never cheated on her and I never would.

'No, thank you, Delisa,' I said. 'I'd rather be alone tonight.'

'I don't mean to insult you,' Delisa sighed, 'but, God knows, so would I.'

chapter nine

Standing on the pavement watching the buses navigate the clutter of bicycles, cars and jay-walkers on Calle 23, I realised that getting to Margarita's shop wasn't going to be easy. Carlota knew Margarita from somewhere, and had arranged for me to talk to her. Over the telephone, the beauty parlour owner said I simply had to hop on a Number 45 *camello* (camel, the Cuban term for the humpbacked public transport buses welded out of converted trailer trucks) and I'd be at her place in twenty minutes. The *camellos* were jammed, and the swarming Habaneros outside looked a lot happier than the passengers sagging in the airless heat inside. I waited and waited, gazing with a swelling sense of frustration at the Number 45 buses pulling up to the curb. If there was no room on a bus and an empty taxi didn't cruise by, what was I to do, flag down a cyclist and beg him to convey me to Margarita's on the handlebars?

And then I saw it, a *camello* with only a half-crowded aisle. I rushed to the door along with a wave of other people. I squeezed, gently pushed, stepped on a foot. When Number 45 pulled away, stranding many would-be passengers in its wake, I was the delighted possessor of an onboard position. I paid the twenty centavos fare and, spying a vacant seat, slid between two men and eased on to it.

'Pardon me,' the middle-aged man standing squarely in front of me said, 'you can't sit there.' He nodded towards the sign above the seat. The space was reserved for pregnant women.

I glanced up and down the aisle. All of the passengers in the immediate area were male. 'I'll get up the moment a pregnant woman gets on the bus,' I pledged.

'You must understand,' the man said harshly.

'Understand what?'

'It isn't right for you to be in that seat. Don't force me to report you. You'll be thrown off the bus.'

I loathed the prospect of waiting on the pavement for another Number 45, but the man was an idiot. I stayed seated. He stared cold-faced at a spot over my right shoulder for the next twenty minutes, and when the rocking *camello* pushed his leg against mine, he jerked it back as though it had brushed a nuclear-waste container.

Entering Margarita's shop, I broke the conversational ice by telling her about the guy on the bus.

'Bureaucrats!' she wailed. 'That *camello* goes to a big government office. Rules are rules. You can almost see it stamped on their foreheads, seeping through from their brains!'

With a feisty opening like that, I figured I was in for a daringly blunt interview. Margarita settled beside a potted plant in the closed shop – she shut her doors every Thursday, her district's electricity-saving 'blackout' day – and switched to a more cautious mode, a condition familiar to foreign writers questioning small-scale entrepreneurs receiving the government's blessing.

Since the government lifted its ban on free-enterprise ventures in 1993, thousands of Cubans have launched such capitalist businesses as repairing electrical goods, owning restaurants and selling produce at farmers' markets. One vendor at Havana's Marianao Market quit a 300-peso-a-month teaching job to earn 1,000 pesos a day peddling his own brand of marinade.

Diving into capitalism's uncertain waters had also been a winning move for Margarita. She declined, however, to reveal the extent of her prosperity, or where she obtained the start-up funding, or how long she was a seamstress before enrolling in a hairdressing course. Those were, she said, personal matters, and she couldn't see why she should expose them in print. She did say that her annual licence fee was $5,000 and, obeying the state law forbidding the employment of non-family members, her husband and two daughters were on the salon payroll. Even queries that were inanely shallow that I should've been ashamed of myself for asking ('Do Cuban women prefer curly or straight hair?') drew evasive replies. As the interview limped to the finish line, she suddenly pitched caution aside.

'Are you planning to expand your business?' I asked.

'With their permission, I will.'

'With whose permission?'

'The bureaucrats!' she flamed. 'I've got three dryers and business is good and I want two more! I filled out the papers for permission to install them five months ago! Five months ago! The bureaucrats are choking me!'

Margarita's resistance to discussing her life more fully disappointed me. I wasn't at all surprised, however, that the notion of governmental bureaucrats touched a nerve so raw that she temporarily lost her reticence. In the years I'd been travelling to the island, I'd heard countless Cubans deliver similar lashes to the invisible physique of the nation's most

popular whipping boy, the insensitive, uncrushable civil
service.

Bitching about bureaucrats was a universal compulsion
that didn't have quite the same meaning elsewhere as it did
in Cuba. Only the lion-hearted or swaggering fools openly
criticised Castro by name. Jail terms averaging six months
were levied against ordinary citizens found guilty of uttering
what could be interpreted as anti-Castro remarks; an
estimated 1,000 men and women belonging to outlawed
pro-democracy groups who blatantly bad-mouthed El
Comandante were serving prison sentences ranging from
one to eight years. To prevent possible repercussions, in
everyday conversation people stroked their chins, a visual
reference to Castro's beard, instead of saying his name.
Respectful supporters sometimes called him El Lider, El
Jefe, El Comandante and Abuelo (grandfather) while
disrespectful non-supporters dubbed him Señor Tege
(Mister Blah Blah) and Tía Tata (which translates roughly
as Aunt Nursemaid).

Unwillingly to risk punishment, Cubans tended to blame
almost everything that failed in their society that couldn't
be attributed to the American blockade on the faceless civil
servants. They were apparently a safe target for verbal abuse
because Castro himself had criticised their general
inefficiency. 'The civil service cannot enter the twenty-first
century clinging to mid-twentieth century methods,' he said
in a 1990 National Assembly speech. 'The civil service …
must streamline.'

Marching to the leader's beat, the Assembly approved a
plan to speed up the bureaucratic process by slashing 50
per cent of national and provincial party slots. The bloated
bureaucracy lost weight, but the overall impact on the

average Cuban's lifestyle wasn't that great. There were still more typewriters than computers in government offices, more adding machines than pocket calculators. It still took six weeks to have a telephone repaired, and up to five years to have an order for a new brassiere filled.

Holidaying at a resort outside Santiago a few years ago, I got my introduction to bureaucracy whipping.

It was raining heavily, and wandering the corridors seeking a giftshop, I came upon a recreation room. A bridge game and Spanish lessons were in progress. A young woman I'd said hello to on the beach beseeched me to play ping-pong. The table looked new, but the paddles and balls weren't lying on it. We searched the room without finding them. I stopped an off-duty waiter passing through the room, a handsome, easygoing youth I'd exchanged dining room quips with. He was a bilingual Cuban whose diplomat father had raised him in the United States. I asked if he happened to know where the paddles and balls were stored.

'Sure,' he answered instantly. 'At the airport.'

'The airport?'

'Yup. The table got here last summer and somebody drove to the terminal to get it. According to customs, our papers covered importing the table, but not the paddles and balls. We couldn't have them.'

'You're kidding.'

'No way. The customs guys were scared shitless of getting their butts kicked for doing something wrong. They demanded an official document from a government ministry saying that it was OK to release the equipment. The hotel wrote a letter and hand-delivered it to the ministry in Santiago. Now our letter's shuffling from desk to desk. Everybody's ducking responsibility. You know what I'm saying? Nobody wants their signature on the approval form. You know what the oldest surviving species are? Cockroaches and civil servants. Both know how to hide and do nothing if there's the slightest chance of trouble.'

'Why did the hotel put the table up if it can't be used?'

'Have you ever been to a resort that doesn't have a ping-pong table? Our manager's travelled the Caribbean and he says he hasn't. We have to have one, just to look like we're really modern, really on top of the wave. I didn't tell you this, by the way. I'm not supposed to tell guests negative shit. I'm always forgetting that talking to people here isn't like talking to people in the States. I gotta watch my tongue.'

'Do you suppose the equipment will ever clear customs?'

'Sure. Eventually. Along with the pillows. I'm sure you've noticed the ones in this hotel are stuffed with cotton batten. Lumpy mothers. We ordered six dozen Canadian pillows, chicken feathers or whatever you stuff in your pillows up there. Anyway, they're collecting dust in an airport shed. Together with the deckchairs and beds we ordered to replace ones that broke. These are all separate shipments needing separate documents. A bureaucratic hell.'

Years later, driving a rental car, I picked up a married couple in their forties on the highway north of Santiago. They had got a ride from Havana and were hitch-hiking the last thirty-five miles to the city. The husband didn't say much, and when he did speak, the words came in short, loud, hard blasts that reminded me of the power tool that mechanics tighten wheel nuts with. The woman, on the other hand, was a wordaholic whose soft voice belied a combative demeanour.

It was the woman who thumped the bureaucrats.

The couple were planning to open a restaurant and six of

the seven permits they required cleared the public service hurdles. They had been to the capital to visit a childhood friend who had once worked in the head office of the government department controlling the permits. They had hoped that he might contact a former colleague and speed the final licence through the labyrinths. The friend had enlightened them that the civil service was no longer the corruption-free system it had long prided itself on being. The economic nose-dive following the Soviet pull-out resulted in a small minority of bureaucrats soliciting bribes. One of Castro's sons, Fidelito, was rumoured to have been dismissed from the nuclear energy ministry for illegally pocketing money.

The couple's request for their friend's help caused him to hum and haw and finally divulge his secret. He was frightened to contact his old civil service colleagues in case his reappearance flicked a light on in somebody's head. Several years earlier he had had abdominal surgery, and as a special favour, the department commanded the payroll branch to send his regular cheque to his residence. He recovered his health and, accepting a job in a private company, he resigned from the government post. Someone either forgot to notify the payroll staff or the termination documents were lost. Whatever the reason, he had been receiving and cashing cheques in spite of a recurring nightmare in which he was lying on the floor, bound and gagged, in a spider-infested prison cell.

'Our trip was for nothing,' the power-tool voice blasted in my ear.

'Horrible,' his wife said. 'It's depressing to discover the bureaucrats aren't just stupid, they're becoming crooks. I'll never bribe anybody. It's counter-revolutionary. If you take a bribe in China and you're caught, you take a bullet in the brain.'

'Tell him your joke,' the man said. 'He'll know how much this country hates bureaucrats.'

'A policeman handed an ordinary citizen a pistol and three bullets, and ushered him into a room. Adolf Hitler, a baby-murderer and a Cuban civil servant were handcuffed to chairs. The policeman instructed the citizen to shoot them. The citizen walked over to the bureaucrat and fired three bullets into his skull. "Why did you do that?" the policeman asked. "You were supposed to kill all three." "Please forgive me," the citizen said. "I'm Cuban and I just wanted to make sure the bureaucrat was dead."

That was a piece of intentional humour. A week before I visited Margarita's salon, I was shown an example of the unintentional kind. I had gone to a flat in suburban Havana to talk to a white-haired, bespectacled poet about the deceased author he idolised. His literary hero wasn't Martí or any other Cuban writer; it was Ernest Hemingway. The grand master of romantic activism had lived in a farmhouse outside Havana from 1939 until 1960. Both Hemingway's hillside dwelling and two Havana bars he frequented, the swank El Floridita and the hole-in-the-wall La Bodeguita del Medio, were government-run tourist shrines. He meant to return to Cuba – he committed suicide in Idaho in 1961 – and he had left the house fully furnished. Books, letters, war souvenirs and a glass-topped writing desk are among the items displayed. According to the poet, the burly novelist did do his drinking at the two bars, but the well-known handwritten Hemingway note exhibited at La Bodeguita – 'My mojito en La Bodeguita, my daiquiri in El Floridita.' –

was the forged handiwork of a post-Revolution tourism bureaucrat.

Our conversation glided from the Hemingway shrines to a job the poet used to have writing government brochures. It was a frustrating experience. Everything he wrote was screened by a band of upper-echelon bureaucrats. Shaking his head, the poet said, 'Those people weren't writers, and yet they deemed themselves capable of editing the material. None of them possessed the vaguest notion of how inept the changes looked in print. Here, let me show you.'

He retrieved a road-safety pamphlet.

I read, 'If you are driving during the night and wish to smoke, light your cigarette with the vehicle lighter. Although the damage won't be permanent, matches may blind you.' Then I read, 'It is advisable to brake your vehicle if it is descending a hill fast.' Upon reading the third safe-motoring recommendation, I burst out laughing. 'If your vehicle spins out of control and races towards a solid object, such as a wall, remain alert.'

The poet shook his head again. He took the pamphlet from me and returned it to a dresser drawer. 'Our GNP has dropped thirty-five per cent since 1989,' he said in a sour tone. 'That's the year the Soviet bloc began to disintegrate, and the bloc was our biggest trading partner. For nearly forty years Cubans were guaranteed lifetime employment. It was actually a crime not to be employed. Now the government's started laying off hundreds of thousands of workers and we're seeing something new in this city, men hanging about, existing on social assistance cheques. Perhaps I'm cynical, but I doubt many senior bureaucrats will be thrown out of work. The sardines end up in the frying pan, not the barracudas.'

blue cuban nights

The Castro regime's financial dilemma had worked to the advantage of international companies. In the early 1990s the dollar-starved government altered its investment laws and allowed foreigners to share ownership of commercial enterprises with state corporations. Canadian, German, Spanish and Latin American firms steered money into tourist-area hotels and pizza parlours, as well as manufacturing and mining projects. In 1995 the law was revised and foreign firms were accorded sole ownership rights, although only twenty-five-year leases were sanctioned in certain cases. The following year, after Cuban MiGs downed two 'Brothers to the Rescue' aircraft (an American organisation that helps Cubans fleeing their country), killing four civilians, the American government passed legislation that discouraged an inestimable number of companies from doing business in Cuba. The legislation punished international companies operating there by banning employees and their families from entering the United States: it also paved the route for Cuban Americans whose property was confiscated during the Castro dictatorship to sue foreign owners in US courts for compensation. Defying the American legislation, about forty Canadian companies continued to invest in Cuba, pumping hundreds of millions of dollars into the economy since the Soviet collapse.

Bringing hard currency didn't render the foreigners immune to the bureaucratic curse. A Spanish hotel chain, Guitart, reportedly fled a joint venture deal in frustration over a lengthy red tape entanglement. A German businessman considering opening a joint-venture restaurant in Varadero said he loved the Cubans' friendly and eager attitude, but he was astonished by a Cuban bureaucrat's view on the businesses' mandate. The bureaucrat opined that the restaurant didn't have to be profitable, that he was aspiring for it to employ a dozen Cubans, pay its taxes and break even. For Delta Hotels, a Toronto-based chain contracted to manage a new state-owned hotel, the problem wasn't a bureaucrat's paltry ambition. Fish caught in waters near the building were trucked to a distribution centre in Santiago, forty-five miles south, and then shipped back to the hotel. By the time the fish arrived it was no longer fresh. To skirt a state law forbidding foreign firms to make their own monetary arrangements with the locals, Delta and a team of government officials hammered out a solution: the Cubans created a fish co-op close to the hotel.

Ian Delaney, CEO of an Alberta-based resource firm, Sherritt International, has stressed that patience is an essential virtue when dealing with Cuban officials. Sherritt's wholly owned nickel-mining operation near Holguín was the outcome of almost five years of negotiations. Those discussions included six-hour dinners and lunches with Castro.

Not every investor had Castro for a meal companion, but lengthy dining room conferences were common. A Canadian manufacturer told me he spent numerous two- and three-hour luncheon sessions talking to civil servants. 'The Cubans aren't revved up commerce machines, the type of time-is-money characters you'll meet in Canada,' he said. 'They chat about their children, sports and world affairs and ask you a hundred questions about life in Canada. It's fantastic, really. Maybe they're slow and overly cautious when it comes to signing contracts, but you get to know them as human beings.'

While deploring the civil service's glacial pace, Castro has nonetheless said he understood the necessity for caution. During a heated National Assembly debate in 1995 on whether sanctioning 100 per cent foreign ownership of companies on Cuban soil would corrode socialism, El Comandante stated he had personally met 'idiots, swindlers' bearing 'false offers and papers proposing all sorts of nonsense.'

Deep-sea diver Glenn Costello may have seemed a nonsense-bearer to some civil servants. The Halifax native landed in Havana in 1993 proposing that he be granted the right to salvage treasure-packed Spanish galleons sunk in Cuban waters. He endured a 31-month bureaucratic ordeal before the Cubans consented to a specific project. Costello's sponsoring company and the government would split the loot fifty-fifty upon recovery of seven ships sunk in Matanzas Bay four hundred years ago. In a *Saturday Night* magazine article, Costello said the bureaucratic conferences led to shouting matches and slammed doors. 'The Cubans are typical Latins,' Costello said. 'Machismo is everything ...'

Shouting matches and slamming doors are cathartic experiences most Cubans deny themselves. Scorning bureaucrats in private is one thing, singling yourself out as a troublemaker and a possible anti-Castroite by engaging in face-to-face confrontation is another. Still, there is an appreciable degree of satisfaction to be had in a private denunciation.

One cloudy afternoon Roberto and I were on La Rampa, the downtown Havana street that sloped towards the oceanfront. Ahead of us, walking purposefully, Roberto spotted a comely, frizzy-haired woman of around forty. He knew her by sight; she was a department head in the national rationing ministry. She had done something Roberto disapproved of to a friend of his.

'Are you familiar with the Cuban expression, *"Ella está infumable"*? ['She is unsmokable.'] We say that about an ugly woman.' He pointed at the bureaucrat. 'That woman has a cute face, but she's unsmokable.'

We began to discuss the Mexican film we were going to see at Cine Yara and stopped paying attention to the bureaucrat. When we saw her again, she was standing in a doorway holding one of her shoes; the heel had snapped off. Roberto went over and described the route to a repair shop. The woman thanked him, then hailed a bicycle-taxi.

'I'm a disgusting person,' Roberto said with satisfaction. 'There's no shoe repair on Calle 21.'

What Roberto had done was infantile and mean-spirited, but in a nation where any manner of victory over a bureaucrat, large or small, is regarded as a feat, it wasn't my place to admonish him.

chapter ten

In the summer of 1960, while the Castro warriors were taking stock of their freshly won kingdom, Juan José Pérez was passing a sunny Monday morning doing what he normally did on weekday mornings: pushing a rubbish cart along a sleepy Miramar street. From time to time he paused to collect a scrap of paper, a banana skin, rubbish that blemished the posh neighbourhood. The Revolution had brought new tenants to the sumptuous mansions, replacing fleeing or arrested Batista apostles, but from a street sweeper's point of view, nothing had changed. The newcomers thoughtlessly dropped the same amount of rubbish on the pavement as their predecessors.

Juan halted to light a cigarette in front of a large white house with arched doorways, leaded-glass windows and a tiled roof. Through the iron fence, he saw a well-groomed man and his equally well-groomed wife load baggage into two taxis. Both ignored Juan's inquisitive stare. He was obviously of no consequence to them, a black man in a drab uniform, leaning against a rubbish cart. The couple loaded the first taxi with suitcases and after cramming more luggage in the boot of the second, summoned three children from the house. The man didn't lock the door. The taxis scooted off and Juan picked up his broom again.

That evening, Juan caught a bus to Miramar. The mansion was wrapped in darkness. He slipped inside. The electricity was off, the phones were disconnected and the rooms were bare except for mattresses and bedding on the bedroom floors. On Tuesday morning he contacted a housing committee official. Juan said he had heard new Miramar tenants were paying low rents and he politely suggested that since the Revolution was for everybody, he should be able to move into the vacant house. The official looked up the address. The owner had scampered off to New York. In a haughty letter to the government, he said he wanted the house to stand empty until the Revolution failed in a year or two and he could reclaim it.

'The Revolution is for everyone,' the official advised Juan. 'The poorest of the poor are masters of the mansions these days. No one's applied for that house, señor. Move in before they do.'

The following Monday, when Juan rose to go to his street-sweeping job, he rose in the mansion he and his family were calling home.

That had all happened more than forty years ago. Now, enfeebled by an incurable blood disease, Juan José Pérez lay in an upstairs bedroom of the Miramar house, his skin as dry and brittle-looking as aged parchment. Like a child recalling his happiest Christmas, he sparked with a sense of excitement when he related his story.

'Fidel Castro got us this house. Fidel Castro. And he got the Negro respect. Fidel Castro, he was Moses. He guided us to the Promised Land. Yes, he did. Guided us to the Promised Land. He was on the TV and said the Negro was the same as the white man and shouldn't be kicked no more. Don't say nothing bad about Fidel Castro in this house. Anybody does, they aren't welcome.'

Juan wasn't alone in his glorification of Castro as a Moses-like hero. Millions of Cuban blacks owed their workplace status and freedom of personal movement to equality policies implemented during the revolutionary regime's first year of power. Castro's empathy for blacks was genuine, a surge from the heart and not a case of shrewd political pandering. Abraham Lincoln was among his boyhood idols, and he had been immensely influenced by his reading of Harriet Beecher Stowe's anti-slavery novel, *Uncle Tom's Cabin*.

Perhaps more significant, although these things cannot be accurately judged, was his revulsion for his father's attitudes and actions. Angel Castro despised blacks. He had come to Cuba as a Spanish soldier fighting against an army comprised largely of former slaves fed up with colonial rule. Taking advantage of a law granting white settlers free agricultural land, Angel Castro finished his military service and established a plantation in predominantly black Oriente province. In his 1988 book, *Castro, The Blacks and Africa*, American sociologist Carlos Moore described the elder Castro as a brutal disciplinarian whose favourite pastime was shooting at blacks as though they were rabbits. History did not record whether the young Fidel, a word glutton unimpaired by self-doubt, dared to challenge his father to a racism debate. It did record that Angel Castro and other light-skinned Cubans continued to abuse blacks with impunity long after slavery was abolished in the 1880s.

Prior to Fidel Castro's entry on the leadership stage, black Cubans were forbidden to cross the thresholds of certain cafés and private clubs or to set foot on specified beaches. Offices and shops declined to hire them, and only the sleaziest hotels rented them rooms. The blacks permitted on the streets of upper-crust districts like Miramar were servants, tradesmen and public service workers.

Penalties for disobeying the unwritten law could be harsh. Sometimes the police beat the interlopers, sometimes members of the Kuban Ku Klux Klan meted out their own brand of punishment, terrorising 'rebellious Negroes'. In 1933 several supposedly unbiased newspapers printed a KKKK policy statement decrying the mixing of racial strains. 'Our organisation believes the two races existing in Cuba should exist separately from each other,' the statement said.

The legal system wasn't a training camp for KKKK recruits, but it may as well have been. In 1942 the mayor of Havana scoffed at the notion that he was encouraging anti-black behaviour; opposing the mayor, Miguel Angel Céspedes, a private club president, stated, 'The courts in Cuba are the first to discriminate against the Negro.' Two years later, a Havana judge dismissed a discrimination charge against a beauty parlour manager who refused to do a black woman's hair.

Cubans loath to associate with blacks weren't opposed to appropriating one of the most bedazzling elements of black culture, the yearly carnival. During slavery, the Spanish authorities created King's Day, an annual event in which singers and dancers attired in African costumes paraded in cities and towns to the ancestral rhythms of drums, rattles and trumpets. Provincial governors stood on palace balconies throwing coins into the crowd. The carnivals continued after slavery was abolished. Around the turn of the century, Havana society figures, staging a white version of the parade, restricted the black carnivals to the poorest barrios. Extravagantly costumed whites rode along the Malecón and the elegant Prado Boulevard in horse-drawn carriages and on flower-covered floats. The Second World War ended the whites-only tradition. To draw tourist dollars, Havana merchants persuaded civic politicians to bring the vastly more enthralling black carnivals back to the main streets in 1946. (The splashiest annual blow-out nowadays is a five-day carnival in Santiago de Cuba that pays homage to Santería gods.)

Castro's insurgents pledged equality for blacks in their outlawed Radio Rebelde broadcasts. Black community leaders pressed Castro not to forget that promise soon after he set up shop in Havana; the black soldiers fighting for independence in the 1800s hadn't improved their lot under the new white rulers. Castro was true to his word. In April 1959, he made a nationally televised address in which he vowed racial discrimination was finished in the schools, the labour force and society in general. 'We are committing the crime of not granting work to the poorest elements of our community. Colonial society turned the Negro into a slave and gave him no remuneration. Our society refuses to allow him a decent living. The coloniser worked him to death, and beat him to death, and we force our black brothers to die of starvation!'

Castro's impassioned commitment demolished walls for blacks, but the racist beast was hard to kill. 'Santiago isn't a pleasant city to visit,' a housewife told me offhandedly. 'It's full of blacks.' A mathematics professor said all of Cuba's AIDS victims were 'immoral black musicians.' And a journalist's wife insisted, 'Negroes have supernatural powers. Never look one in the eye. You'll be cursed with ill luck.'

As for the black community, there were grumblings of tokenism within the Party hierarchy. Blacks held prominent bureaucratic positions, but none were invited into Castro's inner circle. Many people referred to a prominent army general as El Negro, instead of by his name. The flood of mostly white Cubans to Florida had whittled down the light-skinned majority: by the mid-1990s, the country was 51 per cent mulatto, 37 per cent white, 11 per cent black and 1 per cent Chinese.

What did Juan think? Was racial prejudice in Cuba a larger and crueller animal than I felt it was?

Skipping over the question, Juan said, 'He's a hero to me.'

'Fidel Castro?'

'Him, yes, but it's José Martí I mean. José Martí. That's his picture.' The Martí photograph, tinted and sun-faded, was encased in a decomposing plaster frame. It faced a wall adorned with family pictures and a Santa Barbara medallion. Juan and his now deceased wife had conceived eight children; a son and a daughter and their four offspring now lived in the house with Juan. 'Martí was for the Negro. He said the Negro was suffering greatly, and the greater the suffering, the greater the need for justice.'

'How severe is it now?' I tried. 'Do blacks encounter much prejudice in everyday life?'

'I won't talk about that.'

'OK.'

'It's personal. In my family, we don't say nothing to each other about it, and I won't say nothing to you. Every human's got a cross to bear and mine's being coloured. Talk to Felicia. She teaches school. She isn't shy, she speaks her mind. I can't read or write. She reads books and she sees white people all the time. She'll set you right.'

Felicia was Juan's granddaughter. Diminutive and neat,

she had the tired, burdened look that teachers wore like a universal identity badge. She was on the veranda, sitting on a wicker swing peeling an orange. A blue and yellow-striped lizard scurried up a laurel tree. Did Cubans eat lizards? Feeling she'd be offended, I let the question slide by unspoken.

'So did my grandfather tell you the Vatican should canonise Fidel Castro?' was Felicia's tongue-in-cheek greeting.

'Saint Fidel. I read somewhere that ninety per cent of Cubans are Roman Catholic. Canonisation might be a popular move.'

The swing was big enough for two, but glancing at the badly rusted chain, I seated myself on the blue-tiled edge of the veranda. The yard was spacious and weedy. Past a disused stone fountain spider-webbed with tiny cracks, the family had planted a herb garden and installed chickens in a wire-mesh pen.

'I forgot to ask your grandfather. How much rent do you pay?'

'Ten per cent of the family income. That's the standard rent every Cuban pays.'

'Wow. That's pretty good.'

'Before the Revolution half of my grandfather's salary went to renting a filthy apartment with cockroaches and rats and halls smelling of the chemicals the landlord sprayed to get rid of them. Most of the tenants were blacks and mulattos – even if they had the money, no one but a tenement landlord would rent them a place.'

'Now you can go wherever you want. The cafés – the beaches –'

Felicia swallowed an orange segment and said, 'On paper,

we have the right. But who's got the cash to eat in restaurants? Not many blacks. The beaches – well, we don't go to the resorts the tourists go to. The plainclothes police watch us like hawks and we're uncomfortable. But there are three hundred beaches in our country and it's no problem finding one where we feel all right.'

Historian Rafael Duharte Jiménez contended in *AfroCuba*, an anthology examining black culture published in 1993, that the past discriminatory practices were based on fear. Educate blacks and award them basic freedoms, and they were bound to strive for social domination. The nineteenth-century Haitian slave revolt strengthened the white populace's view that Cuban blacks needed to be kept under heel. Agreeing with Duharte Jiménez, Felicia said the fear of blacks, a single-headed monster in the 1800s, had grown a second head over the generations.

'Black women were a taboo and white landowners, forbidden little else in their privileged lives, secretly bedded them. Mulatto children were born. I can't remember the year – the middle of the last century – a novel called *Cecilia Valdés of Angel's Hill* was written. The novel's famous here. Cecilia Valdés was a mulatta vixen. A beautiful, brainless virgin. She seduces a wealthy white man's son and causes him grief. White Cubans were scared of mulatto assimilation in those days and they are even more scared now. There are six million mulattos. What drives the purebreds batty is the fact that many mulattos can pass for white.'

'Somebody swore to me there's a cream that mulattos use. It allegedly lightens their skin and increases their chances of winning a white Cuban's affection.'

'*Mio dios*. If they are buying the cream, they're wasting

their money. Nothing short of divine intervention can change skin colour.'

Felicia slid off the swing and went to the chicken pen. The feathered captives darted forward to peck at the orange peel.

Felicia rested on the swing again. 'What did you say? Oh, racial prejudice. No, I don't know whether it's widespread. The discrimination legislation forced the hard-core bigots to slither into underground holes. I do run into one of them occasionally. Nothing serious. Nothing like this atrocious woman when I was a child. My mother was in a tourist shop seeing a friend working there, and I wandered around looking at the clothes and candies and cans of soda pop. This woman, a nose-in-the-air Spaniard, dropped her handkerchief on the floor. I scooped it up and handed it to her. She was outraged. "You little animal! I'll have to throw this away now that your little black hands have touched it." It was a dagger straight to my heart. I've never forgotten her cold eyes and the hatred in her voice. I pity the black people she's run across.'

Felicia's children arrived home from a special outing to a research laboratory. A boy and a girl, handsome and frisky. They flung cotton school bags on the kitchen table and, laughing and squealing, chased each other about the house. Felicia got up to attend to them. 'I enjoyed our conversation,' she said.

'Me too.'

'I'm surprised you didn't ask about the chickens. If we're raising them for sacrifices. Carlota said Santería fascinates you, and that you're going to Trinidad tomorrow to question a priest.'

'Are you?'

'Am I what?'

'Raising chickens for witchcraft?'

'No, señor, we're not. Putting curses on your enemies has its merits, but in this house, we'd rather have the eggs.'

chapter eleven

The shattered glass was lying in the third-floor hallway. Bits and pieces of a green wine bottle. Coming out of my room, I stepped around the glass. Going up to a maid who was plucking crisp linen off a cart, I mentioned the hazard.

'I clean rooms,' she responded. 'I don't clean halls.'

I tried reaching to the depths of her maternal soul.

'Children run up from the beach without shoes. The glass is dangerous.'

'I'll have it done,' she said coolly. 'All right, señor?'

The maid's attitude was in keeping with that of other people on the hotel staff. Waitresses clustered in the furthest alcove of the dining room, chatting in subdued voices and avoiding patrons until they got up from their tables to summon them. The rental manager offered no consoling words or apology to an upset German woman whose scooter took its own life, forcing her to push the dead machine five miles along a shadeless backroad. A desk clerk rejected a guest's request that he change rooms to escape a dripping air conditioner that was robbing him of sleep. A master of work-ducking invention, the clerk said a provincial law made it illegal for guests to switch rooms.

Apathy travelled the hotel corridors like a body-numbing wind. The source was easy to identify. The hotel was wholly owned and operated by the Cuban government. Everyone was paid the same salary, waitresses and maids, rental managers and clerks, and with no performance bonuses or wage increases tied to promotions, there was no incentive to labour hard and suck up to the guests.

I went to the ground-floor dining room. The previous night's dinner had been a memorable combination of spaghetti and sauerkraut. Today's breakfast fare consisted of boiled eggs, hard toast and the sauerkraut remains. I ate the eggs, left the sauerkraut for a noon-hour diner to savour and, putting myself on full-throttle alert, drank three cups of exquisite Cubita coffee.

Trinidad was twenty minutes from the hotel. The taxi travelled past an estuary and an abandoned cement factory and through dusty streets rimmed by squat, threadbare, hot-looking houses. The suburb shrank and vanished as the taxi climbed a steep hill leading to the centre of Old Trinidad. At the summit, the town wore its charms proudly, like centuries-old porcelain, cracked and faded, yet still able to attract and enthrall. Although several of the colonial buildings were intricately restored, most were crumbling. Narrow balconies jutted above cobblestone streets and cast-iron cannons, seized from seventeenth-century pirate ships, were planted muzzle-down and transformed into hitching posts. A tourist museum behind the square exhibited turn-of-the-century glassware and furniture unwillingly contributed by the town's ruling class following the Castro uprising. Near the museum, two men stood at tiny stalls selling cigars, chocolate bars and packages of coffee. Down the hillside, a pair of low-key government souvenir shops viewed each other across a quiet street. Trinidad was that rarest of survivors, a world-class beauty spot uncontaminated by fast-food and disco pollution.

I was rendezvousing with a Santería priest in the main

square. I was nervous, and it wasn't because of the breakfast coffee or a fear of his supposed supernatural connections. I had forgotten to ask my Havana contact if Ramón worked with snakes. Earthly sinners are, I suspect, eternally confronted in Hell with the thing that they dreaded most in life. For some, it's a tax audit that never ends or the sound of an accordionist playing Wagner. For me, Hell is copying Indiana Jones' descent into a reptile-filled chamber. Upon reading that Jean-Paul Sartre theorised Hell was other people, I surmised there weren't any snakes in France.

I waited beneath a royal palm. Neither it nor its equally tall companions had benches near their bases. What was the point when the locals wouldn't sit on them? They insisted the trees conveyed bad luck – over the years, they said, numerous people had died in their vicinity. Lightning caused some deaths; other people suddenly dropped dead on clear, warm days. A Catholic priest had laughed at the royal palm superstition, and to show Trinidadians their beliefs were idiotic, he had leaned against a tree during a horrendous rain storm. He didn't perish, but he was shaken; lightning struck an adjacent palm, hurling a big-leafed branch to his feet.

I didn't know whether the royal palms were responsible, but in the twenty minutes I was there no one entered the square. Then a woman in a brown dress crossed the road and walked up to me. A mulatta with a round face and kind eyes, a sweet-scented flower in her hair. The Santería priest had dispatched her to guide me to his house. She piloted me down side streets, past residences with balustered windows that opened onto cool parlours and plant-dotted interior patios. The tiles on the sloping roofs, the woman explained, were shaped by slaves. They sat in the sun in a factory yard with wet clay drying on their thighs.

'Slaves and pirates,' the woman said. 'That is our history. Pirates kept families in Trinidad. Some of the mansions here belonged to people trading in contraband. Did you see the tower in Sugarmill Valley? Five storeys! A sugar baron built it to imprison his unfaithful wife in a room below the bell. A cruel monster, he was. Cruel as a scorpion. He was sure the ringing would be so bad she wouldn't cheat again. Not a doubt in his stupid brain. He released her from the tower after eight months and she immediately seduced a new lover. She had grown to cherish the bell – she'd go to the tower room to listen to it!'

'Bizarre. Does Ramón use snakes in his ceremonies?'

'Never! Are you frightened of them?'

'Terrified.'

'Pick one up and you won't be frightened anymore.'

'A friend said that as he handed me a garden snake.'

'Did you touch it?'

'I realised I should, but it's impossible when you're jumping head-first over a fence.'

Owing to its slave origins and supernatural doctrine, Santería was limited to peasant communities for generations after a Nigerian tribe, the Yoruba, transplanted it to the sugar cane fields in the fifteenth century. The wealthy elite scorned the religion and the Roman Catholic Church tried to eradicate it. To combat persecution, Santería avoided a high public profile. It still does to a certain extent. There are Santería shrines and Celina González recorded an enormously popular song about a Santería god, 'Long Live Changó', but there are no mass pilgrimages to sacred sites, no door-to-door salvation sellers. Appropriately, Ramón's home was indistinguishable from others in the district. The whitewash was old and dull, the iron window-grills disintegrating.

'Go inside,' the woman said, cutting me loose. 'He is ready.'

There wasn't a stick of furniture in the ante-room. Blue waves, clouds and stars were painted on the walls. White sun and moon symbols decorated the concrete floor. I descended four steps into the living room. A corner altar held a plaster replica of Yemayá, a black goddess. There was a Cuban flag, a framed snapshot of a youthful baseball team, a Russian television set and a wreck of a bicycle.

Ramón walked in from the patio. A tall, sturdy figure attired in a white shirt and trousers, he had an energetic, self-assured gait. I was reminded of a renowned cellist I had interviewed at her parents' suburban home. She had come into the front room in a similar manner.

Ramón's hand gripped mine confidently.

'You are safe here,' he said. 'The chains buried under the steps keep demons out.'

'Good.'

'Would you like some coffee?'

'No, thank you. I've had three cups already.'

Ramón smiled. 'Three? By this hour of the day, a Cuban has had ten.' He sighed and added, 'Those Cubans more prosperous than I am.'

We started with the altar. Yemayá protected mothers, he said, but worshippers directing their prayers to her were also aiming at a cloth-wrapped stone near the foot of the shrine. The stone was sacred and believers must never see it. Ramón nodded towards the water glasses, fruit and bread laid out on a table. The water and food were to satisfy the thirst and hunger of deceased relatives. A cauldron beside the table contained a machete. A dead man's soul inhabited the cauldron, Ramón said, and the machete was there to defend it. Ramón showed me a coconut shell carved into a crude impression of a human face. The face represented Eleggua, a god governing destiny. The gods and goddesses Santería followers worship are nature oriented. Changó was in charge of fire and lightning, Oya the wind, Oshún the rivers and Oggun farming. Some served additional roles. Changó, for instance, was also associated with dancing and battlefield prowess.

Two weeks earlier, over lunch at Havana's Hotel Nacional, a Cuban journalist had told me he was amazed at how many of his friends who used to ridicule Santería had become devotees.

'Catholicism was our god and it is failing to fulfil our needs,' he'd said. 'Communism is failing the people too. Santería promises to deliver things, spiritually and materially, that the Church and the Party are unable to provide.'

The reporter claimed top-ranking military officers and civil servants pay regular visits to Santería priests and priestesses. While they are better off financially than most Cubans, they are feeling the hard pinch of economic restrictions. True or not, a Cuban story, passed from mouth to mouth for decades, has it that Castro defeated Batista because he visited a Santería shrine and wrapped a statue in combat fatigues. His enemies whisper that he retains power by practising black magic to crush opponents.

'I won't comment on those matters,' Ramón says. 'I am a solid Communist and I will not discuss Fidel and his politics.'

'What about the Catholic Church? Will you discuss that?'

'No problem.'

'Is the Church trying to suppress your religion?'

'No, not anymore. But it doesn't adore us. Some Catholic priests declare we are a superstitious cult and not a true religion. Yet there are bishops urging the Vatican to totally accept us. They say the Church cannot expand and flourish unless it fully embraces Santería, which has millions of followers in this country. Catholics have been known to reject the Church if their parish priest refuses to stop attacking Santería.'

When the Church attempted to wipe the religion out during the sixteenth century, sacred objects were hidden beneath replicas of Catholic saints. Out of these deceptive measures, a hybrid religion emerged. Catholic traditions such as a belief in Jesus Christ and the Virgin Mary became part of Santería teachings. So did the dispensing of holy water; *santeros* (Santería priests) disdain the Catholic policy of selling it to the masses, professing that its magical powers were vastly reduced when holy water was distributed like a commercial product.

'Is it possible to be both a fervent Catholic and a fervent believer in Santería?'

'Of course. Catholics attend church in the morning and visit *santeros* that afternoon. What do they pray for? The usual. Improved health, a job change, a lover's fidelity, material objects like a bigger house. You have an expression in English, "hedging your bets". That is what they are doing. Hedging their bets.'

We heard someone come in from the street. Ramón greeted a handsome, wide-shouldered woman whose short blonde hair had recently taken a peroxide swim. A boy, roughly six years old, was attached to her hand.

'I'm sorry. I shouldn't be interrupting,' she said uneasily.

'No problem,' Ramón said. 'Do you want to talk now or after this gentleman leaves?'

'Now. It's urgent. It's Carmelita Rameriz. Her children are ugly.'

Ramón nodded. 'Yes, I know. I've seen them.'

'Her sister sends clothes from Hialiah. She drapes her girls in fancy blouses and dresses, and scrubs their faces until they glow, and they're still ugly. Look at Alfredo. Isn't he pretty? Women will throw roses at his feet.'

Alfredo raised his chin and smiled pleasurably, as if his girlish countenance was an award-winning portrait he'd painted.

'Carmelita Rameriz insulted Alfredo?' Ramón asked.

'Worse. This morning she stopped me in the street. She patted Alfredo's head and said he was a beautiful child. She said, "It would be a shame for him to be stricken with a deformity."'

'A curse.'

'It felt like it. I trembled like an earthquake.'

'Wait here, señora.'

'Please hurry. This is urgent.'

Ramón went into the adjoining bedroom. The woman removed a handkerchief from her purse, spat on it and bent over, studiously wiping the child's brow and cheeks. A silver crucifix jumped over the top of her blouse and dangled. She kissed it, crossed herself and tucked it in. Fate had presented an ideal demonstration of mixed Vatican-Santería allegiance.

Ramón returned with a glass eyeball in his hand. He pinned it to the underside of Alfredo's shirt, over his heart, and announced it would defend the boy against Carmelita

Rameriz's evil-eye curse. The grateful mother dropped coins in his palm before departing.

I asked Ramón if he ever put curses on people. He was offended.

'Never,' he snapped. 'Four generations of my family have been *santeros*. We didn't learn this in school, we didn't go into it simply to feed our families. The spirits choose us to create white magic. We weren't chosen to do black magic.'

I hung around a bit longer, inquiring about the herbal medicines the *santeros* dispensed. Ramón said he had cured insomnia, liver ailments and arthritis. That very morning he had prepared a herbal concoction for a fisherman's wife anxious to eliminate her husband's dandruff. At the door, I brought up black magic again. He promised to set up a meeting for the following day.

'Señora Gómez is a *bruja*,' he said. 'The English word is "witch". She is a daughter of the night. A widow no one dares to marry. Men are frightened. Her husband was very robust. He hit her and called her obscene names and all of a sudden his health collapsed.'

'Thank you for seeing me today.'

'My privilege. Oh, one more thing. Take her a photograph of someone you dislike. She will render a curse.'

I got to the hotel around two o'clock. I went straight to the dining room for a meal of fried eggs and fish of an unknown lineage, maybe grouper. A pair of young Vancouver males occupied the next table, scuba divers with sculpted bodies.

'I didn't know Cuba was Communist,' one of them said. 'When did that happen?'

'The sixties,' his companion answered. 'Jesus, Harvey, don't you listen to the news?'

'Yeah, sometimes. If I'd known they were here, I would've gone to Hawaii. Communists make me puke.'

Upstairs, the maid I had spoken to earlier was lifting the broken bottle into a bucket. A holidaying Mexican woman, a yellow and red beach outfit covering her rotund frame, was standing over her demanding, not requesting, that she remove every shard and splinter. She was, I guessed, a lady accustomed to pressuring underlings.

'The major will fix her wagon,' she said to me in fluent English. 'The government's fed up with inefficiency. The military's taking charge of hotels. A major's coming to whip this dump into shape. Spit and polish. Slackers beware. This little girl –' she scowled at the maid, a woman in her mid-thirties '– will be dancing to a brand-new tune. Have you eaten downstairs? The menu's a joke. Chefs are trained to cook meals their teachers – men spending their entire lives eating rice and beans – decide tourists crave. We get soggy potatoes and toast hard enough to raft to Florida on. The major's bringing a new chef. A Frenchman. Next month this girl will be hopping.'

In my room, I switched on the television. Without satellite and cable, which the pricey foreign-operated resorts supply, channel choices were minimal. I watched five minutes of a Cuban documentary on a nickel-mining project and ten minutes of a Spanish-dubbed version of a black and white Western, *High Noon*. I had brought magazines to disperse to Cubans famished for uncensored information. *Newsweek*, *Vanity Fair*, *The Economist*, *Premier* and *People*. I leafed through them until I found a suitable photograph for Señora Gómez.

The next morning, I made my way to her house. She lived on a street that had a certain notoriety. At one time, it had been a pirate domain. There was a river behind the north-side houses and when Spanish soldiers raided the area, eager to arrest them, the brigands jumped into small boats and floated to the sea.

Standing at the witch's door, I hesitated. I wasn't sure I really wanted to do this. I didn't believe in black magic, but what if I was wrong? I might be consigning misfortune to a man I'd never met, destroying something he valued. On the other hand, I empathised with Carmelita Rameriz. Wishing the physically perfect to suffer was, loathsome as it may be, a normal sentiment.

I knocked.

chapter twelve

I half expected Señora Gómez to proximate my vision of a hinterlands witch, an overweight hag with dirty fingernails and a morose disposition. She was, in fact, slim, tiny and disturbingly attractive. Voluminous black hair expounded on the glories of a fashion style deserving global resurrection, ringlets. Her appearance wasn't the only surprise. She embroidered. Cotton flowers and horses enlivened the rooms. An embroidery hoop bore the makings of a cotton sailboat. Nothing anywhere suggested she practised the wicked arts.

'I don't understand why Ramón sent you to me,' she said in a gentle voice.

'I'm interested in black magic. He doesn't do that.'

'Perhaps he doesn't, but his *santero* colleagues do. I am not a member of their clan. I belong to myself and no one else. Did he tell you all *santeros* detest black magic?'

'He implied that.'

'What a puppeteer. He was manipulating you to write nice stories. The truth is, *santeros* are as much dreaded by the masses as they are respected. Not too long ago, babies were stolen from mothers and sacrificed at Santería rituals. Worshippers drank babies' blood. Now, chickens are sacrificed. Now, chicken blood goes down their throats. *Santeros* are not as noble and innocent as Ramón pretends.'

She was barefoot. She sat on a rocking chair and pulled

on ragged sneakers. She said we were going for a walk in the hills. She hoped the heat and mosquitoes wouldn't bother me. Would there be snakes? She shook her head.

'The little terrors respect me. My power dwarfs theirs. Even the three-step knows I can turn it to dust.'

'I haven't heard of the three-step.'

'The most poisonous snake in Cuba. It bites you, you take three steps, you keel over dead.'

We proceeded to a road outside Trinidad that trailed over an unpopulated hill carpeted with thick underbrush. If I were a three-step, I'd hide there, napping and snacking on insects until I got a quick thrill fanging a passer-by. On the other side of the hill, we walked across cane fields. The sun had the sky all to itself but sea breezes routed the mosquitoes and the heat.

'I shouldn't have spoken harshly of Ramón,' the witch said. 'He has a courageous spirit. Trinidad isn't very big and everyone will know of your visit. In the past, *santeros* were killed for speaking to non-believers. The older *santeros* continue to dwell behind barriers of silence, and Ramón will be severely criticised.'

In contrast to the four-generation *santero*, Ramón, Señora Gómez did not tread in her ancestors' footsteps. Her father was a postal clerk, her mother a cannery worker. Both were Protestant. As a child, she was anguished by nightmares and sporadic hallucinations (demons appeared in the family kitchen and in the school yard). At ten, Señora Gómez's parents took her to a mountain village to spend time with her widowed grandmother. A child had been killed. The little girl was stolen from her bed and found the following day near the river. Her body was torn apart.

'There were tales of child killings in other mountain

villages,' Señora Gómez said. 'Years and years in the past. So long ago that only the oldest of the old people remembered. My grandmother said that someone in the village must have killed the little girl, the lunatic relative of the lunatic man who had killed the other children. The villagers said no, it was a wild animal. It climbed through the window and carried the little girl off. The villagers said it hid in a cave and came out in darkness. My mother made me sleep in the bed with her. I couldn't go anywhere alone, not even the outhouse behind my grandmother's. In my dreams – my nightmares – I saw demons and monstrous beasts and petrified little girls.

'On a Sunday, we were walking by the river, my mother and me. Some men were sitting on the ground, talking and smoking. My eyes fell upon a thin young man. He was laughing and teasing his friends. My blood went cold. I saw something – I knew he murdered the little girl. I told my mother. She knew I had the gift of special sight. The villagers ridiculed her story, but they agreed to question the young man. He confessed. He begged them to end his misery and they beat him to death and buried his body. What did I see at the river? I saw the wicked truth. I saw he was a werewolf.'

In her thirteenth year, Señora Gómez was capable of implementing evil-eye curses, and at eighteen she apprenticed to a ninety-year-old witch. The witch had a house in a Santiago barrio and Señora Gómez's parents, respecting their daughter's burgeoning abilities, arranged for her to live with an aunt.

'That old *bruja* was crippled in one arm and almost blind, but she did things I can't do. With time, yes, but not now.'

'What kind of things?'

'A mother came to her with a dead baby. The old *bruja*

slept with the baby in her room overnight. In the morning I heard the baby crying and when I got up, the old *bruja* said, "Fetch the mother. The baby's wet and it isn't my duty to change its diaper." She did magic in her home but I won't do that. My private life's separate. There aren't any spirits in my house. Yet I have horrible sleep. I'd be overjoyed to dream a happy dream someday.'

We reached a derelict building. A one-room dirt-floor shed. The door hung on a single hinge. The witch lifted the door aside and we stepped over the threshold. Clumps of dried leaves, flowers and grass dangled from ceiling nails. I saw animal bones and skulls, candles, black necklaces and needle-pierced dolls. A vulture stood in a corner, quiet and almost motionless, an ankle chained to a post.

Señora Gómez touched a doll. Glasses and a moustache were painted on the expressionless face. 'He is finished,' she said. 'Soon he will go to his mistress and swagger like a big man. Then he will learn his blade doesn't cut bread.'

'I'm not sure I understand.'

'For his wife, I rendered him impotent.'

'How?'

'I burned pumpkin leaves and an undergarment of his. A rat was sacrificed. But it is you we are here for, not this man. Who do you wish to punish?'

I gave her the magazine photo. She viewed Richard Gere's impeccable features without a flicker of recognition.

'Usually, I don't have a photograph. Only a name written on paper. Photographs are stronger.'

'What will you do?'

'Force the vulture to eat it. Then torment the beast. When it dies, the man in the picture dies.'

'Oh.'

'Isn't that your desire? Ramón's message said you were seeking a powerful curse. I understood that to be a death.'

'Ramón's message was misleading.' I had thought she'd be amused when I disclosed the victim's identity and stated what I had devised for him, but in that small space, the tools of her dark trade all around us, amusement was impossible.

'Wait outside,' she said.

I positioned myself beside the doorway and glanced sideways.

She deposited the picture in a bowl and placed dried leaves and white powder on top of it. Crouching and glowering, she muttered what may have been an incantation. The vulture looked sleepy. Why was it so passive? Was it drugged, was it caught in a devilish spell? Señora Gómez rose, and speaking softly, she addressed a black doll set apart from the others. Then she walked outside.

'That wasn't very long,' I said as she adjusted the door.

'More later,' she said. 'How much did Ramón charge you?'

'Nothing.'

'I can't afford generosity. One *yanqui* dollar will please me.'

'OK.'

'*Santeros* live off the fees clients pay them and every time they accept those pesos, they are conducting a business without a state licence. The police don't arrest them, the police don't jail them. The clients confess secrets to *santeros* and the *santeros* whisper those secrets into police ears. I'm not saying Ramón's spying or that every *santero* does, but some do. Yes, yes, some definitely do.'

We returned to Trinidad. On the hill, descending towards

the road, she referred to a doll I had missed. A teenage girl dreamt she had committed suicide after her father's boss raped her. The father judged the dream to be prophetic. Señora Gómez coiled a ribbon around the neck of a doll bearing the boss's resemblance. The boss was expected to hang himself before the rape could occur. 'I am not always successful, but you'd be surprised how often I am.'

Richard Gere sped to mind. If she succeeded in his case, how guilty would I feel when the tabloids transmitted the news that his teeth had sadly and mysteriously fallen out?

chapter thirteen

Roberto dipped a spoon in the sugar bowl and floated it to his mouth. He swallowed the sweet substance, licked the spoon and tilted the kitchen chair back.

'How was Trinidad?'

'Great. I met a witch. She put a curse on somebody for me.'

'Who?'

'Richard Gere. The film star.'

'I've heard of him. He screwed Cindy Crawford. Actors have curses on them already. That's why they're actors and not real people. Who runs their life making believe they're other people? Lunatics. The cursed.'

'Is she a real person?' The snapshot of Alicia Alonso was amongst a dozen pictures attached to a cork bulletin board. The ballet legend was instructing a group of female dancers at a rehearsal; dressed in black, she was slight, intense and vivid, a concentrated mass of bones and determination.

'Ask my mother,' Roberto said. 'I don't know her and I don't want to. Ballet's dead. Alonsokov drags its decaying carcass around the country, but the young don't care. Rap. Rock. That's all they want.'

'What did you call her?'

'Alonsokov. She's such a good Communist – endlessly yapping about Russian culture – that we've awarded her a Russian name. She's a fantastic dancer, nobody says she isn't, but she cosied up to Batista and she cosies up to Fidel. A lousy opportunist. If she wasn't, she'd be living in Miami.'

The criticism against Alonso and other artists who declined to go into exile wasn't new to me. The sniping started with the banning of Orlando Jiménez Leal's documentary, *PM*, in 1960. The government censors ruled that scenes depicting urban nightlife – Habaneros boozing, scrapping, enjoying bar-room music – were anti-revolutionary. Shortly afterwards, Castro stated that artistic endeavours gaining government approval would support Communist ideology. Literary journals were closed down and painters and writers were arrested for defying the edict. Before he fled to New York, Reinaldo Arenas wrote, 'Communism is a species of Catholicism. The difference is that whereas Catholicism proposes a choice between heaven and hell, Communism proposes only hell.'

Novelist Guillermo Cabrera Infante migrated to England; film director Jiménez Leal, cinematographer Néstor Almendros, trumpeter Arturo Sandoval, vocalist Celia Cruz and hundreds of lesser-known artists joined the exodus. Yet Cuban culture was awesomely rich, and despite being shackled by a restrictive system, it continued to grow and sparkle. Tomás Gutiérrez Alea directed his most stunning films, *Death of a Bureaucrat* and *Memories of Underdevelopment*, under Communism. Visual artists produced extraordinary work, Silvio Rodríguez became an immensely popular singer-composer, jazz pianists Chucho Valdéz, Gonzalo Rubalcaba and Hilario Durán sharpened their talents.

It was, I ruminated, unfair for Roberto and his ilk to criticise artists for not seeking exile. Many remained in Cuba because they were hard-core socialists. Others stayed for family reasons. When a Cuban citizen travelled to a foreign land, he or she was obliged to leave their spouse and children on the island. If they defected, the chances of their spouses and children receiving permission to follow them were extremely slim. In a milieu where blood relationships were traditionally valued above financial and social prestige, no one deserved to be sneered at for not choosing artistic freedom over family.

As Roberto scooped up a second spoonful of sugar, I asked him whether his mother shared his negative assessment of Alonso.

'How should I know? We don't talk about ballet. She knows I couldn't care less. Delores is the one she talks about ballet with. Balanchine, *Swan Lake*, crap and more crap.'

'Is Delores your sister?'

'Yes. My precious, adorable sister.'

Finally, her name was spoken. There were pictures of a tall, long-haired girl on the corkboard whose broad mouth was a reissue of Carlota's. She was, I deduced, the daughter Rosa said Carlota had. But neither Roberto nor Carlota mentioned her and I had stifled my inquisitiveness, fearing I'd touch a raw sore. Carlota's daughter was likely a *jinetera*, seriously ill, shacked up with a vile man or entangled in some other horrific situation the family faced with silent resolve. Now Roberto had broken the silence, opening a window I immediately dived through.

'I've never seen your sister. Where is she?'

'Away. Listen, Ted, my mother wants to explain about Delores. Why she doesn't talk about her. She thinks you must be wondering. She's been waiting for the right time.'

'What exactly is the problem?'

'I'll let her tell you. Aren't you meeting my mother tonight? Bring it up then. While she's filling her face.'

For ice cream lovers like me, the open-air Coppelia outlet in the Vedado was, dowdy appearance notwithstanding, the grandest of pleasure palaces. Day and night, six days a week, hundreds of customers clustered in the big, tree-shaded square to delightedly consume what was, in my immodest opinion, the world's most delicious ice cream. Under Prío and Batista, Havana's finest ice cream parlours were whites-only establishments selling twenty-eight varieties of Howard Johnson ice cream shipped from Florida. Terminating the Howard Johnson contract, Castro commanded the food minister to come up with a selection list rivalling the American company's. The experts exceeded their mandate. More than fifty flavours were introduced at Coppelia, and to Castro and the rest of the population's gratification, the Cubano ice cream tasted better than the *yanqui*. Coppelia was such a prized institution that when West Germany stopped sending butter and milk (it no longer needed the cattlefeed Cuba traded for those items), the government severely cut back dairy-product sales in Cuban stores in order to supply the chain. Coppelia was as vital to maintaining public spirit as '*Patria o Muerte*' (Country or Death) billboards and the adulation of sports stars. On the evening I went to the square with Carlota, there were long lines leading to the ticket booths and the counter where the tickets were exchanged for dishes of ice cream. Some patrons had been waiting for over an hour; on Sundays, the waiting period was up to five hours.

'Forget the line,' Carlota said. 'There's a special section for *turistas*. Go to the ticket booth and flash your passport.'

'I can't. It's in a safety-deposit box at the hotel.'

'Your driver's licence, flash that.'

Feeling guilty about jumping the line (but not guilty enough to refrain), I obeyed Carlota's instructions. The era of fifty-odd flavours had passed, but the four menu items that night were sufficient. We sat at a small table in the general seating area; I didn't want to risk being drawn into a dialogue with a guy in a Blue Jays cap telling me what the weather was like every day of the week before he boarded the plane.

Gays, and men and boys renting their bodies to gays, hung around the square at night, defying police harassment. The table closest to us was occupied by two young males gazing fondly at each other; one of them was a full-blown drag queen. Carlota sized up the couple and apparently decided they weren't liable to call the police to report anybody's conversation.

Making a beard-stroking motion with her hand, she said, 'He adores Coppelia ice cream. He ate ten scoops at a time before his doctor said he had to lose weight. He doesn't smoke cigars anymore. The doctor said they were fouling his lungs.'

'Fidel hasn't looked good in recent photographs.'

'He's got a weak liver but he'll live to be a hundred. He's a genius trying to improve the lot of his people, and the gods reward those kind of geniuses with longevity. How old was Mao when he died? Over eighty.'

'Do you think Alicia Alonso will have a long life? She's an artistic genius.'

'I pray she does. She's earned it.'

'Roberto isn't a fan of hers. He calls her Alonsokov.'

Carlota looked pained. 'That child of mine, he doesn't understand. Alicia Alonso does whatever is necessary to ensure the ballet survives. Dance is beauty. The price for presenting beauty to the masses is aligning herself with the ruling party – capitalist, Communist, whichever badge it wears – and she will pay it. Roberto should be at a factory when the ballet performs there. Let him witness the workers' shining eyes, let him hear the loud applause. The people appreciate dance, they praise Alicia Alonso for destroying the barrier. Before 1959 the lower classes weren't allowed in Coppelia. The ballet was off-limits too. Now everyone and anyone comes to Coppelia. And when Alicia Alonso brings dance to a factory yard, or a sports arena, or a town plaza, it doesn't cost one person a single peso.'

In a corkboard photograph a pubescent Delores, cheeks heavily rouged, raven hair held by a ponytail ribbon, posed in a dance costume. Was she following in her mother's slipper steps? Roberto had stated that his mother wished to discuss her daughter; this seemed a good time.

'Is Delores going into the ballet?'

'No, she'll be a teacher,' Carlota answered reluctantly. So reluctantly, in fact, that I nearly regretted inquiring.

'Is something the matter?'

'It hurts me to speak about her. I'm worried sick. She isn't a strong girl. I said she couldn't do physical labour, but she passed the medical examination and there was nothing I could do.'

Delores was sixteen. Under Cuban law, university education was free, but students were required to toil one month each year on a rural work brigade. Delores was helping harvest tomato crops somewhere east of Havana, a dawn-to-dusk activity that, as much as it concerned Carlota, wasn't as daunting as the fate awaiting her daughter the following winter. Through the grapevine, Carlota learned that because she had challenged the system by attempting to have her perfectly healthy daughter excluded from the tomato-crop mission, Delores was going to be handed a worse assignment, a coffee-picking brigade. In February she would be bused to a rainy, isolated mountain range. The coffee was grown at high altitudes and the pickers rode up and down from base camp in aged vehicles on narrow, often slippery dirt roads. Lacking adequate rain gear, many workers became ill and were treated by a nurse who had little medicine at her disposal. Some pickers were injured and others were stung by scorpions. At the base camp, they slept in dormitories and went unwashed when the bathroom facilities gave up the ghost. The meals generally consisted of buns for breakfast, soup for lunch, and rice and beans and a banana for dinner. Being young and energetic, many students regarded coffee-picking assignments as invigorating challenges. Delores wasn't among them. She was too delicate to do well at physical labour, and she despised communal living. Carlota hadn't informed her yet that she was on the coffee-picking list and when she did, the girl was expected to be terribly anguished, perhaps depressed.

'I blame myself for this,' Carlota said.

'It was out of your hands. In Cuba children belong to the state, they don't belong to the parents. You aren't responsible for a decision the state made about Delores.'

'Yes, I know, but I was stupid. I made a fuss. I wrote a letter and I yelled at a government man I shouldn't have yelled at. I'm a Cuban cannonball. I explode. Maybe that's the reason Cubans eat ice cream. It cools them down.'

I thought that was the end of it, that Carlota had finally told me what she wanted to tell me. Months later, in the deep freeze of a Canadian winter, I was to discover that the most wrenching and saddest part of Carlota's story was yet to unfold.

We took a bus to Carlota's neighbourhood. Neither of us were tired. She filled two glasses with home-made wine and we went up to the roof. Carlota's decrepit block of flats was tall enough to provide a panoramic view. Not that there was a lot to see. To save electricity, many streets and buildings were unlit. Here and there, candles and kerosene lamps burned. The darkness around us was thick, muggy and, I swear, had a bluish tinge.

'It reminds me of one of Pablo Neruda's love poems,' I said. '"Naked, you are as blue as the Cuban night."'

Carlota nodded and said, 'He's drunk.' She was observing a man on an adjacent rooftop. He walked unsteadily to the edge and stood peering down at the street. 'If he jumps, the bureaucrats will be furious. He doesn't have an exit visa.'

'Didn't a cabinet minister kill himself on television?'

'On television? No, I don't believe so. Wait. You're thinking of Eduardo Chibás. A long time ago, in the fifties. It wasn't television, it was radio. He was the opposition party boss when Carlos Prío was president. He accused Prío of scandalous deeds and then he yanked out a pistol and shot himself. His last words were, "I'm dying for Cuba."' She chuckled and said, 'Crazy country. I don't understand why I love it, but I do. I couldn't live anywhere else. Roberto dreams of Miami, but I don't. Cubans are miserable in Miami. Their dream is coming back here.'

I envied Carlota's sense of belonging. In all likelihood, it is a common characteristic of children who know they are adopted to grow up feeling separated from the rest of society.

I had lived in various Canadian cities and my global travels included three years' residing in a Mexican hill town. I never felt insecure, not a day in my life; I was at ease wherever I stayed, and yet I had never experienced anything similar to Carlota's soul-deep conviction that she was in her spiritual home, the terrain she was meant to inhabit.

The man on the adjacent roof turned and wove his tipsy way to the exit door.

'It's hard to be sure in the dark but I think I know him,' Carlota said. 'He's a *gallego*. The same as Miguel.'

'What's a *gallego*?'

'A light-coloured person.'

'Then you're a *gallego* too.'

'No, no. There's more to it. *Gallegos* trace their families back to the Spanish province of Galicia. They're stubborn-headed, and they feel superior. The ruling class. El Comandante's father came from Galicia. Did Miguel speak about the blue eyes? His eyes are brown, but for generations the people in his family were blue-eyed. A sign of racial superiority. I'm curious – how did you two meet?'

We met, I told her, in Costa Rica. My wife and I were on holiday and Miguel was on government business. The hotel was owned by a bald German whose private residence was protected by a huge, snarly dog and a porch-sitting bodyguard of similar description. On a balmy afternoon, strolling up from the beach, Jessie and I stared at the house and exchanged completely groundless remarks, speculating that the owner was fugitive Nazi war criminal Martin Bormann. Unbeknownst to us, Miguel was walking close behind. He chimed in, saying we were mistaken, it wasn't Bormann, it was the Führer. Out of those moments of feeble humour, a friendship blossomed.

What I didn't reveal to Carlota was that Miguel's brother, Luis, had showed up at the hotel. Defection tales were verbal minefields. Distorted in the retelling, the innocent may appear to be guilty. Miguel was ignorant of his brother's intention to persuade him not to return to Cuba, but should the tale pass from mouth to mouth, as many accounts did, it might end up implying that he encouraged the scheme, changing his mind at the last moment. Luis had defected years earlier and was raking in piles of cash peddling real estate in Florida. He had obtained a false Mexican passport and he beseeched Miguel to use it and fly to the States. Luis had Cuban government contacts and Rosa and Vicente could eventually emigrate. Miguel said no, he believed fervently in the Revolution and wasn't ready to desert it. Typically Cuban, the brothers fought noisily, flinging insults and accusations and, typically Cuban, they hugged and cried and kissed beside the taxi taking Luis to the airport.

'Do you still go to Costa Rica?' Carlota asked.

'I never went again.'

'Isn't it beautiful?'

'Beautiful but dull. The music's wimpy, the politics are boring, there isn't a writer worth reading. There are toucans and monkeys and glorious flowers, but it's a country without literature, without an exciting history. It has no depth, nothing to engage the imagination.'

'I read in an American magazine that Cuba was dull. A big, gloomy prison where we shuffled sullenly about as though we were dragging heavy chains. Big liars! Even in chains, Cubans would be dancing. When Machado was in charge – and Prío – and Batista – we didn't shuffle, we held our heads up.'

I knew little about exiled presidents Gerardo Machado

and Carlos Prío Socarrás. Machado's favourite device for controlling his enemies was, I had read, having them gunned down and Prío, a campus agitator who helped end Machado's murderous reign fifteen years before he himself became leader, was buried near his old foe at Miami's Woodlawn Park Cemetery. Both men were heroes to Batista, an army stenographer and the country's champion speed-typist, but his admiration for Prío didn't halt him from ousting him from power.

It was true that Castro's Communism tried in its early stages to bleach the colour out of Cuba. The vast majority of his countrymen understood and accepted the need for bland uniformity, but they resented some limitations on their personal freedom. Smuggled copies of banned novels were circulated throughout the island. When yet another '*Socialismo o Muerto*' sign appeared near his home, a Havana attorney denied the right to move his practice to Santiago blackened the 'o' and altered the sign to read, 'Socialism = Death'. Two students were arrested for doing the Twist in Parque Central; a farmer went to court to unsuccessfully defend his right not to surrender his tractor to the state. Recognising that the people weren't programmed robots and needed some glamour in their lives, especially the variety enhancing their sense of national pride, the government copied the Soviet model. Millions of pesos were poured into amateur sport. Medal-winning athletes flew home from international competitions to the rapturous cheering and applause of airport crowds.

The patriotism-geared sports machine produced an extraordinary individual in the 1990s. Sprinter Ana Fidelia Quirot shattered two world records, capturing gold medals at the 1991 Pan American Games, then followed those performances with a bronze-medal run in the 1992 Olympic Games. With her sculpted physique, braided hair and charming smile, Quirot was a photogenic contrast to the grim, mannish-looking female athletes the Russians crafted. Then fate delivered a cruel package to her doorstep. A kerosene burner blew up in Quirot's Havana flat: she suffered third-degree burns to 40 per cent of her body and lost her unborn baby. Plastic surgery, physical therapy and a gargantuan amount of grit and willpower took her to the point doctors predicted she'd never reach – at thirty-three, she sprinted again, reaching second place in the 800-metre final at the Atlanta Olympics.

Ana Fidelia Quirot's story was anything but dull – and neither was the country she was born in.

'What magazine was the article in?'

'I can't remember,' Carlota said. 'American.'

'Was it *Reader's Digest*? The editors despise Communists.'

'I don't know. It was a big, big lie. Americans think Cuba's gloomy because we don't have McDonald's and silly video games. In the United States of America you lock your doors, and bar your windows, and lie in bed praying the children next door won't take drugs and kill you. Guns everywhere, and everybody's scared they'll drive their car down a bad street in a bad neighbourhood. You tell me, my Canadian friend, which country's a big prison – America or Cuba?'

chapter fourteen

'Take off your sunglasses,' Delisa said.

'Why?'

'We don't have glasses that fancy in Cuba. If they think you're a foreigner, they'll stop you.'

'I thought you said there wouldn't be any problems. You're friendly with the guards.'

'There won't be. But it's better to be on the safe side.'

I removed the identity-revealing shades and stuck them in my shirt pocket. The sun blasted through the car window; I blinked, squinted and focused on my knees. Delisa parked her boyfriend's Nissan and we walked to the sanatorium entrance. Shielding my eyes with my hand (a gesture clearly indicating I wasn't a sun-immune Cuban), I read the gate sign: *No Dejar Entrar* (Keep Out). There wasn't a guard in view, disputing the rumours that armed soldiers with ill-tempered dogs patrolled the grounds, and part of the rusting chain-link fence hung free from the post.

'Rafael is *muy simpatico*,' Delisa said, adjusting the strap of her imitation Chanel handbag. 'He was a boyfriend of mine. Years ago, before I started modelling at El Palacio.'

She had already said that on the phone. She had called the hotel to ask me to post a letter in Canada. It was a thank you message for a Quebec businessman who had sent her an extravagant gift through a third party. She informed me that she was driving to an AIDS sanatorium. Was I interested in coming along? Yes, I responded, I was definitely interested.

Cuba was the first country to round up and quarantine AIDS victims. Roughly 350 patients were housed in sanatoriums, the majority of them in the Havana region. International human rights advocates condemned the quarantine system and nationwide compulsory AIDS testing, and I wanted to know how the patients themselves regarded these measures.

We ducked under the gate barrier. A uniformed guard ambled out of a building, staring at the ground. When he raised his eyes, he called for us to stop. He knew Delisa and he spoke to her flirtatiously. He was glad to set his weary eyes upon her beautiful face, he said, but he couldn't break the no visitors rule. She handed him a packet of Marlboros.

'This is the last time,' he said. 'I'm serious, Delisa. There's a doctor who'd feed my liver to the sharks. Fifteen minutes, and you're gone. Right?'

Rows of low white flat-roofed buildings were assembled amidst palm trees and shaggy, weed-throttled lawns. They looked like converted military barracks. The patients' rooms lined both sides of an inner courtyard; most of the doors were open. Men were reading, listening to cassettes and playing dominoes in the manner favoured by Cuban males, banging down the tiles as though the game's objective was to crack your opponent's pieces. An acne-cheeked youth leaning against a doorframe told Delisa she was an angel sent to sleep with him.

'The day I go to bed with an AIDS case,' she said to me, 'is the day I'll know I'm suicidal.'

Rafael was pleased to see her. 'The guards weren't going to let you in again.'

Delisa shrugged. 'One guard, one pack of Marlboros. Two guards, two packs of Marlboros. One guard today and I've got an extra package. Jorge smokes doesn't he? Give them to him.' She dug the cigarettes out of her handbag, then produced the bottle of rum I had got for her at the hotel. 'Save the rum for yourself. Don't share it with us.'

'You're an angel,' Rafael said.

'What's going on?' Delisa asked. 'You're the second patient in this institution today who's called me an angel.'

'We're dying. Heaven's on our mind.'

'Heaven's on your mind, my dear Rafael, but your neighbour had a less sacred subject on his.'

Rafael's unbuttoned shirt was hanging out. He was uncommonly thin – hollow belly, ribs pressed tight against pale skin – but otherwise he appeared to be a healthy individual. In his late twenties, Rafael retained the keen-eyed, boyish look of a teenager and fittingly, his room resembled a college resident's quarters: a narrow bed, utilitarian table and chairs. Photographs of Winona Ryder, clipped from foreign magazines, brightened a wall. Rafael's tribute to the actress was scrawled in English above the pictures: Our Lady of Perpetual Pretty.

It was a long-standing piece of legislation, the Danger to Society Act, that made Rafael's sanatorium confinement necessary. The country's first known AIDS victim, a soldier coming home from duty in Africa, was diagnosed in 1985. Doctors tested more military personnel, chiefly people who had served in Angola and Mozambique, and the discovery of additional cases prompted the government to open a quarantine facility in 1986. Six more sanatoriums were established in subsequent years. In 1994 Rafael, an actor and teacher, submitted to an AIDS test. A doctor asserted he was HIV positive and a danger to society, and Rafael pledged to report to a sanatorium. He went underground.

'I was mad at the world for not being able to cure me,' he said. 'I slept in deserted buildings and I supported myself by stealing. Breaking into houses, siphoning gas, taking bicycles and stripping them to sell the parts. I mugged a couple of guys.'

'Tourists?' I asked. 'Cuba has the reputation of being the safest Caribbean country to travel in.'

'No, they weren't. Tourists are safe here. Most of their hotels are in the provinces, where the crime rate's low. They're built on beaches, miles from cities and towns, and, for those that are close to civilisation, there are plainclothes police in the plazas and nightclubs, wherever tourists go. Tourists do get robbed, but it's a kid grabbing their beach towel and running. Nothing worth real money. Nothing that inspires professional thieves.'

Rafael ended his criminal career of his own accord. Feeling increasingly sick and exhausted, fed up with bedding down in dilapidated buildings and evading the police, he walked into a Committee for the Defence of the Revolution office and proclaimed he was ready to be quarantined.

He never regretted it.

'The patients here understand one another. We have compassion. Somebody has lesions or he's sick and can't climb out of bed, we don't shun him like his city neighbours would. In Canada you've got Indians, Mohawks and Cree. We're a tribe. We argue, we get depressed, we can't stand the sight of each other sometimes. But we don't lose this sense of belonging to a band. It's tribal. I'm connected to the people here in a way I can never feel connected to people not dying of AIDS.'

AIDS victims were on the priority list for medicine and food, and all of the sanatoriums, from the new, modern blocks of flats to run-down facilities like the one Rafael was assigned to, were equipped with air conditioning. (On the day I visited Rafael, a district-wide power failure had cut off the air conditioning and a workman was repairing the emergency generator.)

The assurance of regular meals was a prime instigator behind the tragic and bizarre actions of a group of disaffected youths known as Los Roqueros (The Rockers). Hundreds of Cubans in their teens and early twenties formed urban street gangs in the mid-1980s. There was a bit of petty thievery and the occasional fist fight between rival gang members, but for the most part the Roqueros were honest and non-violent. Like disciples of a revered spiritual leader, they worshipped American rock music and devoted their entire lives to it. They swapped outlawed tapes, smoked pot and wore their hair long and scraggly. The police, naturally, hounded them ('hippy' hair was an anti-revolutionary offence punishable by a 25-peso fine) and disapproving parents, their own and their girlfriends', gave them the boot. Roqueros yearned for a refuge where they could practise their refractory customs freely. The AIDS sanatoriums emerged as the solution – particularly since the patients were allotted more food than the average Cuban citizen.

Starting in the late 1980s, Roqueros deliberately infected themselves with the AIDS virus. The Public Health Ministry hasn't released information divulging exactly how many youths adopted that ghastly procedure, but unofficial sources estimated the number to be approximately one hundred. The logic behind the self-infection was that well before the disease posed a serious threat to their lives, medical researchers would find a cure. They were also dispatching a shocking statement to the government: the Roqueros believed death was preferable to living without the freedom to be themselves.

In recent years, with the last of the infected Roqueros going to their graves, the authorities noted that the ranks of alienated youths were growing by leaps and bounds and ordered the police to cease hounding them over long hair, earrings and assorted imported regalia. While the government wasn't ready yet to invite Eminem or Slipknot to perform on the island, it was permitting local rock bands to play in public auditoriums.

Rafael had been at a Roquero's bedside when he died.

'He tried to kill himself by smashing a mirror and slashing his wrists,' Rafael recalled. 'A nurse and a patient found him, stopped the bleeding and saved his life. He died a natural death three months later – sobbing and groaning, no control over his bowels, no energy, thoroughly despondent.'

'How did he infect himself?'

'Easy. He got an old syringe from a nurse he knew and went to a friend's house. The friend had AIDS and his father, a doctor, hadn't reported him yet. Sergio filled the syringe with his friend's blood and shot it into his own arm. He did that four times, until he was sure he must be HIV positive. When he went to a clinic, a doctor confirmed that the transfusions were a success. Poor, pitiful Sergio. He was so unhappy that he actually celebrated the day the doctor told him that.'

As the afternoon passed, I half expected the guard to poke

his head through the doorway and chide Delisa for disobeying his edict to quit the premises in fifteen minutes. Passing patients paused and peered inside, briefly mesmerised by Delisa's allure. The air conditioning suddenly whirred to life and a man next door cheered. Then a woman entered Rafael's room, tiny, hawk-nosed, haggard. She was writing a letter for Rafael to a government official, and the paper wouldn't go in the typewriter. I offered to examine the machine.

We crossed the courtyard and went into a room similar to Rafael's. An emaciated man with a long, leonine face lay sleeping in the metal-frame bed. The ubiquitous Che Guevara portrait was centred on a grubby wall while a jigsaw puzzle forming an Alpine meadow, the pieces glued behind glass, was directly across from it. The man in the bed was in his fifties, the woman perhaps ten years younger.

'I've travelled the island,' I commented, 'and I haven't seen a picture of El Jefe.'

'Rare as water in the desert,' the woman said. 'He wants the Revolution to come ahead of personalities. He doesn't want pictures and statues of him everywhere. He isn't a Stalin, he isn't a Mao.'

'Che's picture is everywhere –'

'That's different. He's a dead martyr, and Cubans honour their dead martyrs.' She gestured towards the black Underwood resting on a table. 'My husband's machine. He can fix it but he sleeps and sleeps. The power of the medicine.'

I inserted a sheet of paper and twisted the rollbar knob. The paper jammed. I removed it, and conscious of how scarce paper was, I used the same sheet, trying the other end. It jammed and tore.

'I didn't know married couples could stay in the sanatoriums,' I said, turning the Underwood upside down and gently shaking it.

'You don't have to be married,' the woman said, 'but both people must have the disease.'

The object causing the blockage, a paperclip accidentally dropped into the rollbar, fell out. The fresh piece of paper I inserted sailed smoothly through.

'Is that all it was? Thank you. I'm sorry I troubled you.'

'Does that include homosexuals?'

'Pardon me?'

'Can homosexual couples share a room?'

'Yes. There are homosexuals in this sanatorium. They like it because they can live in peace and be themselves.'

We walked to the doorway.

'Some foreign human rights groups claim it's unjust to separate AIDS patients from the rest of society and lock them up in sanatoriums,' I said.

'A few younger people here say that. But most patients would say the opposite. You show the right attitude – you prove to the staff you won't act irresponsibly – you'll be awarded weekend passes. You can go to your family. You can swim at the beach. My husband and me, we've been out four times since January. We were at our grandchild's birthday last month.' As I stepped outside, she said bitterly, 'It's his fault we're here.'

'Your husband's?'

'Yes. Five years ago, three o'clock in the afternoon, on September fourteenth, he walked in front of a crawling baby. Everybody knows that's bad luck. He's a fool.'

Delisa was on her feet, waiting for me. Rafael was tired and she was heading home.

'Tell me what you need and I'll bring it next time,' she said.

'Nothing,' Rafael said. 'You're a ray of sunshine, Delisa.'

'I've been demoted,' Delisa joked. 'I used to be an angel.' She kissed his cheek and squeezed his hand. 'Take care of yourself, darling. Eat your meals and do what the doctors say. See you soon.'

We strolled to the gate. Two guards were on duty. Delisa stiffened slightly and said she didn't know either of them. 'Don't worry. It won't be a problem.'

The guards stopped us. Delisa retrieved her ID card from the handbag. AIDS victims had the name of their ailment written on their cards: patients accosted by the police for causing trouble during a weekend leave – and those someone reported for engaging in sexual intercourse – were transported to the institution and denied future outings. Delisa's ID passed inspection; she wasn't a patient attempting to flee. The guards scrutinised my driving licence and then permitted me to leave with her. Neither guard questioned our reason for being on the grounds.

'Maybe they thought you were a medical bureaucrat,' Delisa said, climbing into the Nissan. 'And I, clearly, was your mistress.'

I put on my sunglasses. 'How did Rafael get AIDS?' I asked.

'I don't know. Does it matter? He's got it and knowing how he got it isn't going to cure him.'

Pointing the Nissan towards the main road, she said she was driving to her boyfriend's flat to watch videos. He was in the diplomatic corps and had access to such treats.

'I'm moving in with him. His wife hates Cuba and won't live here. He'll fly to her and the kids every six weeks. El

Palacio was firing me anyway. A jealous bitch told them I was sleeping with foreigners. There's a big campaign to kill the sex trade before Cuba becomes a second Thailand. The police are trying to clean up the Malecón. Who cares? That won't stop my sister from whoring. She'll do more nights at the discos.'

'Doesn't the risk of contracting AIDS distress you?'

'Every profession has its risks. What distresses me are foreigners. The government issues sexual conduct warnings and four million Cubans have been tested for the virus, but foreigners are carrying the disease into the country. There are – what's the number? Three hundred, three hundred and fifty AIDS cases now –'

'Three hundred and fifty according to the Public Health Ministry,' I answered. 'With a population of eleven million, I'd be surprised if that number's accurate.'

'Don't be ridiculous. The ministry gains nothing by lying. In fact, if the number was higher, it would be to its advantage. The worse the epidemic, the more people are scared and the more they are scared, the less inclined they are to have unsafe sex. But that isn't my point. What I'm saying is, we are doing a fabulous job of curbing AIDS amongst Cubans, but outsiders are infecting our *jineteras*. We shouldn't allow foreigners past the airport unless they have health certificates proving they've passed AIDS tests. That, I sincerely believe, is the best chance this country has of eliminating the disease altogether.'

I didn't see or hear from Delisa again after that day. Nor did I give the Cuban AIDS situation much thought. Several months after the trip to the sanatorium, on a crisp Toronto afternoon, I was drinking coffee at Starbucks with a friend.

Somehow the conversation touched upon Cuba's approach to the fatal disease. She said the quarantine system was cruel. I said she was mistaken.

'You spoke to two patients and decided everyone loves the sanatoriums,' she said.

'I'm not claiming everyone loves them,' I said. 'It just seems to me that quarantining AIDS victims isn't as awful as you think. Canada quarantines people with other infectious diseases.'

'Well, the Cubans are up to worse tricks. The government's injecting people with the virus. Killing them for scientific research.'

'I don't believe it.'

'It was in the *Financial Post*. They're using human guinea pigs to try and find a cure for AIDS.'

Days later, at a public library, I sifted through *Financial Post* back issues. The story my friend cited was published in July 1996, but she had the facts wrong. A Havana laboratory was injecting forty volunteers with a genetically altered, non-transferable, non-fatal variation of the virus. Heber Biotic president Dr Manuel Lamonte said the biopharmaceutical company had already signed a marketing deal with an Ontario firm. 'If we can produce a vaccine,' he informed writer Peter Morton, 'it would mean tens of billions of dollars every year.'

That, I mused, would be irony in its sweetest form. If the United States was obliged to circumvent its own embargo and purchase a made-in-Cuba vaccine to rescue its citizens from the AIDS scourge, it would, in effect, be holding its nose and vouchsafing prosperity for a regime it was accustomed to treating like a dead skunk on the lawn.

chapter fifteen

Two days after Delisa drove me to the AIDS sanatorium, I boarded a Cubana airline flight bound for Holguín. It was, as they say, a leap of faith. The first time I'd flown to the island in 1986, the Cubana DC7, a dowdy, Russian-built hand-me-down, was delayed lifting off from Toronto's Pearson International Airport. In an unruffled voice, the pilot stated that the entrance door wouldn't shut.

'We have a weight distribution problem. Would everyone from rows A to K please leave their seats and stand in the back of the aircraft.'

Moments afterwards, the passengers reseated, the pilot said, 'Thank you, ladies and gentlemen. The door has closed securely. Providing it doesn't spring open later on, we shall proceed to Havana without further difficulties.'

The second time I took a Cubana plane was for a trip between Santiago and Manzanillo. The door functioned perfectly, but my armrest was missing. The woman sitting beside me speculated that a terrified passenger had heaved himself into the aisle during the last flight, taking it with him. Cubans love recounting horror stories about the airline's antiquated domestic fleet (newer Airbus 320s are now used on international runs), but I haven't heard of Cubana suffering a particularly high fatality rate. Prior to boarding the Holguín flight, I told myself that some of the hugely skilled mechanics responsible for keeping decomposing Nash Ramblers and Oldsmobile 98s on the road were undoubtedly employed as Cubana mechanics. That was my theory, the foundation for my leap of faith.

An hour north of Holguín, a flight attendant climbed on a seat to wipe liquid off a compartment door. 'The air conditioning,' she assured an anxious passenger. 'It isn't fuel.'

The man seated across the aisle caught my gaze and said, 'Cubana's a marvellous airline. Everyone spits on it because the planes are eyesores. Dirt dumb. It's like *putas*. They're old eyesores, you worry you'll get a disease. They're young and beautiful, you don't worry. Real dumb. The next big crash won't be one of these old ladies, it'll be a pretty baby born in a Boeing factory.'

Vicente was waiting at the airport. He was wearing a Miles Davis T-shirt he'd acquired on the black market. He loathed jazz, but the vivid black and white image of the trumpet-blowing musician captivated him. Walking to the near-deserted car park, he said he'd borrowed a sidecar motorcycle to transport me into town. Gossip rolled off his tongue. Ramón and Ana had cancelled their divorce proceedings and moved back in together; Eduardo had quit the radio station to sing in a hotel band; Miguel's schizophrenic poetry editor remained in the mental hospital. Firing up the motorcycle, Vicente said his parents had been overjoyed by the suitcase filled with contraband my wife and I had left behind six months earlier. The medical guides and the aspirin were godsends when Rosa was stricken by the flu; the spark plugs encouraged José's '56 Chevy to perform with renewed vigour. From past experiences, I knew what was in store. Miguel and Rosa would have a gift. I hated taking anything from people who spent every peso with extreme caution, but I understood how important family pride was to Cubans and whatever they'd bought, I'd accept it.

'It's snowing in Canada,' Rosa said, greeting me in front of her house. 'You visit Cuba when your country's frozen.'

'The weather's hot. We don't have snow in summer.'

'No, but your summers are short. The way Canadians speak of winter – the despair in their voices – your country must be a refrigerator eleven months a year. Come in, come in. Miguel will be home from the office soon. People are dropping by later.'

The afternoon travelled a familiar route. I absorbed the tales of family and employment problems and they absorbed my bleeding-heart opinions on how Canadian political and social strife, novel topics for them, should be handled. Miguel arrived late in the day. He participated in conversations, grinning and joking, yet I had an inkling something was off-centre. When the final batch of friends and relatives went out the door, I asked if I was wrong to discuss politics, albeit the Canadian variety.

'No, no. It isn't that,' he answered quickly.

'Then what is it?'

'Vicente drove you straight from the airport. You haven't been to a hotel.'

'No, I haven't. You said in your letter I could stay here.'

'You can, you can. I forgot to mention the hotel. I'm embarrassed to say this. Embarrassed for Cuba. I love her – I'd surrender my life for her – but some things are silly and shouldn't be allowed. Certain rules.'

'Miguel, what is it you want me to do?'

He wanted me to register at a hotel. Not to sleep or eat there, but to have it on record that the hotel was my domicile. It was, he said, an unworkable regulation designed to keep track of Florida Cubans visiting relatives. Sometimes Florida Cubans were on the island for weeks and paid for hotel rooms they never entered.

'You aren't a Florida Cuban, Ted, and I can't say positively that the domicile rule covers just them or all foreigners. Maybe Señora Pérez – the Committee for the Defence of the Revolution's eyes and ears on this street – will report she saw you today and maybe the police will check the hotels. If the law covers all foreigners, there could be repercussions.'

'I can stay in a hotel. I don't mind.'

'No, no. Señora Pérez won't know if you sleep here. It's the registration – it's a necessary nuisance.'

Vicente volunteered to take me to a hotel. We walked uptown. Holguín was a city only the aesthetically impaired might consider, to quote the tourist pamphlet cliché, 'a jewel of the Caribbean.' There were too many plain-faced houses and shops, too many factories producing farm machinery, cigarettes, bicycles and beer. Nonetheless, there was always something to seize your eye in Holguín's lively thoroughfares. On one street a barber was shaving a client who was slumping on a chair in a weedy yard while half a block away, three men wrestled a bleating goat into the back of a battered car. On another street six or seven giggling schoolgirls garbed in red neckerchiefs and white blouses chased a horse cart, shouting mildly worded insults at the driver. Another two blocks and a whistling, white-haired man was sharpening a kitchen knife on a portable grindstone. He sat on a stool outside a cigarmaker's shop, his feet improbably encased in lime-green bedroom slippers.

'My father can be a pain in the ass,' Vicente grumbled.

'The Party is his touchstone. He admits it has its flaws, but he'd let you tear out his tongue before he'd say a political system tailored by a gang of glum Russians doesn't fit fun-loving Cubans. It's like planting orange trees in Moscow. My father doesn't obey the rules because he's scared, he obeys because he thinks everyone should so they won't weaken the Party.'

'You apparently don't agree.'

'I'm not alone, which is strange. My generation grew up knowing nothing but Communism. We went to Communist schools and Juventud Socialista summer camps and ought to have been brainwashed enough to last us a lifetime. The empty shelves in shops, the lack of confidence that things will change, have cleansed our brains. Allow young people to migrate to the US of A and young people would be a rarity in Cuba. Fidel would declare them an endangered species and stick the last few specimens in the Havana Zoo.'

'Does Nena feel the same way?'

'Who knows? That isn't a question you'd put to a woman.'

At the dinner table that evening, eating rice and beans and the tinned Canadian ham I had contributed, Vicente delivered more anti-Communist jabs. His mother wordlessly shook her head and Miguel behaved as if he hadn't heard anything. Around ten o'clock, when Vicente retired to the backyard shed, Miguel attributed his son's remarks to a situation I was unaware of. His marriage plans had been postponed indefinitely. Nena's parents had persuaded her not to wed Vicente until he stopped depending on black market dealing for his livelihood and found a respectable job. With the national unemployment rate climbing, Vicente figured he was doomed to the eternal purgatory of backyard bachelorhood.

Miguel gave me a couple of gifts: a grey and blue striped tie and an English translation of Fidel Castro's famous statement, *History Will Absolve Me*. I hadn't worn a tie since the early 1970s and the instant I saw it, I mentally sank it to the bottom of my sock drawer. The booklet was a different matter. I welcomed the chance to peer into the rebellious head of one of the century's most intriguing political figures.

After Miguel and Rosa said goodnight, I sat in the alcove bed and devoured the fifty-eight pages. Castro had written the text, an address to the courtroom judges, in 1953 while awaiting trial following his forces' abortive raid on the Moncada army barracks. Castro can ramble and bore – his speeches frequently last five hours – but *History Will Absolve Me* sliced to the bone. With fury, righteousness and compassion, he defended the actions mounted against the 'miserable tyrant Batista' and attacked the drastic poverty burdening Cubans. The statement drew upon quotations by Dante, Thomas Aquinas, John Knox and Castro's idol, José Martí, to strengthen its arguments that despotism justified armed rebellion. His mission was, he said, 'the battle of truth against infamy.'

The imagery was electric, and in several instances, a trifle gory. Describing the slaughter of seventy of his captured comrades by Batista soldiers, he wrote, 'Moncada barracks were a workshop of torture and death. Some shameful individuals turned their uniforms into butchers' aprons. The walls were splattered with blood. The bullets embedded in the walls were encrusted with singed bits of skin, brains and human hair, the grisly reminders of rifle shots fired full in the face. The grass around the barracks was dark and sticky with human blood.'

He assailed the agricultural, housing, health and educational systems. More than half of Cuba's farmland was owned by the United Fruit Company and other foreigners. Almost three million homes depended upon candles and kerosene for lighting, and peasant families couldn't afford medical care. 'Ninety per cent of rural children are consumed by parasites which filter through their bare feet from the ground. Society is moved to compassion when it hears of the kidnapping or murder of one child, but it is criminally indifferent to the mass murder of so many thousands of children who die every year from lack of facilities, agonised with pain.' As for the schools the children attended, teachers dipped into their own salaries to pay for supplies, and compared to any small European nation, which financed at least two hundred technological and vocational schools, there were six such institutions in Cuba.

The statement ended with the pronouncement: 'Condemn me. It does not matter. History will absolve me.'

Castro was twenty-eight when the Moncada raid happened. It marked a point of no return for him, the dramatic abandonment of the velvet lifestyle that was his ruling-class legacy. The son of a wealthy Oriente landowner, Castro was a superb scholar and athlete throughout his early school years. He continued to excel at both endeavours after he was sent, at age fifteen, to Belén, the country's most highly valued educational facility. Run by Jesuits, the Havana-based school sculpted the attitudes of upper-crust progeny by, among other character-building tactics, stressing logic above feelings and social ideals over materialism.

Castro later studied law at the University of Havana. Inspired by Jesuit teachings and Martí's political beliefs, he developed into a campus radical, participating in violent demonstrations. When he received his degree, he did what his family expected and settled into the prosperous existence of a suit-and-tie lawyer. He wasn't happy. A former army sergeant, Batista was accepting bribes in exchange for permitting the Mafia to operate gambling casinos. Roughly 15,000 Cubans were working as prostitutes, and untold thousands more were drawing hand-to-mouth wages toiling on foreign-owned farms and plantations. Angry and disgusted, Castro recruited 122 discontented men and women and on 26 July 1953, the rebel band converged in Santiago de Cuba to stage the Moncada assault. The rebels were a poorly equipped force and some pedalled bicycles or rode in taxis to the barracks.

Castro received a fifteen-year sentence for leading the failed insurrection. Two years later, Batista declared a general amnesty and, released from prison, Castro was exiled to Mexico. With his brother, Raúl, and Argentine-born Che Guevara, Castro established a guerrilla training camp in the Mexican jungle. On 2 December 1956, he sailed to Cuba aboard the *Granma* with eighty-one rebels. Only twelve of them survived fierce army attacks.

The tiny band holed up in the Sierra Maestra Mountains near Santiago and engaged in hit-and-run warfare. Word of their heroic exploits spread and hundreds of Cubans, young and old, male and female, came to their camp. The revolutionaries' triumphant march into Havana on 8 January 1959 acquired symbolic significance amongst Santería followers. Dozens of white doves were released during Castro's open-air victory speech: one of them flew onto his shoulder and remained there. In the Santería religion, white doves are linked to Obatala, a deity governing goodness and peace.

Within weeks, Castro set the reform wheels in motion. Radical improvements to the medical and educational systems didn't upset the foreign interests, but other changes did. The casinos and brothels were shut, agricultural land was allotted to more than 100,000 peasant families, and an estimated 150 US-owned businesses were nationalised. The United States behaved as though a child-eating monster was squatting on its doorstep. Eisenhower imposed a partial trade embargo, and in 1961 Kennedy supported a CIA project that involved landing a 1,300-strong force of Cuban exiles at the Bay of Pigs where they were humiliatingly defeated by Castro's forces. Kennedy expanded the embargo to cover all trade goods, and when he ordered the Soviet Union to dismantle its Cuban missile bases in 1962, the world held its breath until the Russians complied.

Sitting in Miguel and Rosa's house, the night deepening around me, I ruminated on Castro and his bucking-bronco ride through history. If he was cut from hero's cloth, as millions of Cubans maintained, the material was flawed. His commendable reform measures were followed by oppressive policing and rigid media censorship. Yet, as dictatorships go, Cuba had a considerably less reprehensible human rights' record than China, Indonesia and Turkey, nations the United States hadn't kneecapped with a trade blockade. I admired Castro for not only standing up to a muscular giant, but outsmarting the giant by downloading criminals and mental patients to Florida during the Muriel boatlift.

His capacity for survival was extraordinary. Only his inner

circle, God and the CIA know how many Langley-born assassination attempts he has eluded. There were rumours that as recently as 1995, a team of mercenaries sprang from a parked van and raked Castro's limo with machine-gun fire, wounding a bodyguard and a chauffeur. Castro guards returned the fire, killing the five attackers. Other assassination plots bore the hallmarks of an evil prankster's handiwork. There were exploding cigars, poisoned inkwells and a toilet seat soaked in a lethal chemical that was reportedly installed in the wrong house.

Adding to the comic opera atmosphere were CIA instructions for Cuban dissidents to undermine the national economy by leaving building lights on and kitchen taps running twenty-four hours a day. In the United States, right-wing columnist Ed Anger reported that a CIA operative had informed him that a dead-ringer impersonator had been filling Fidel Castro's shoes since his death in 1991. 'The dingbat dictator is pushing up daisies in some burnt-out sugar cane field,' Anger told the *Weekly World News*' two million readers.

Neither the chillingly real assassination attempts nor more laughable plots and disinformation tactics have dissuaded Castro. With cunning, passion, *cojónes* and obstinacy, he has remained ringmaster of the longest running Marxist-Leninist show in Latin America. The question was, though, how would his reputation stand up to the scrutiny of recorded history? In other words, in the final analysis, would history absolve him?

I laid the booklet aside and prepared for bed. History may pronounce the Moncada raid justifiable, I decided, but Castro's conduct in power was such a mixed bag of laudable and disgraceful deeds that I wondered who would be able to assess whether the good outweighed the bad, or vice versa. I went to sleep feeling glad that I'd never be summoned to serve on some sort of ethical and moral jury rendering that ultimate judgement.

chapter sixteen

Laura was turning fifteen. She was Miguel's niece, a gaunt, shy girl I'd met but never really spoken to, and yet her birthday celebration was, in addition to seeing my friends again, my reason for the trip to Holguín. Fifteen was the traditional coming-of-age watershed for Cuban females, and when Miguel said in a letter that I had been invited to witness the event, my curiosity flared. I didn't anticipate a primitive initiation ritual – tribal dancers wouldn't be circling her painted body doing the samba while a Santería priest in an eagle-feather headdress carved a fertility symbol on her forehead. What I hoped for was some small insight into the Cuban character. Another door opening into another room.

Tucking the Castro booklet and its dark ruminations into my suitcase, I went into a kitchen rich with yellow morning light. Rosa was frying eggs on the kerosene cooker.

'*Buenos dias*,' Rosa said. 'Did you sleep well?'

'Very well, thank you.'

'Miguel's gone already. He'll be leaving his office early and meeting us at Celia's. She doesn't have a husband, he passed away. Laura's her only child.' She flipped the eggs in the cast-iron pan. 'I don't know if Vicente's going to Celia's. I'll ask when he gets up. I want him to pick up the cake.'

'How would he transport it to the party?'

'His friend's motorbike. That boy worries me sick. Him and Nena.'

'Her parents may relent when they realise how scarce jobs are.'

'It's not that. No, it is that, but it's something else too. He has sex with Nena – I've overheard them talking – but she won't come to the shed and she won't let him touch her in her house. She's scared her mother will walk in. So they go to the train tracks at night. Hundreds of young couples are doing it. Yesterday they said on Radio Angulo that fifty-six lovers were run over lying on train tracks last year. Drinking and having sex and falling asleep. *Mio dios!* Fifty-six dead, and heaven knows how many lost arms and legs.'

'Too bad Vicente doesn't have the money for a motel. That's what lovers do in Canada.'

'There were cheap hotels in Cuba. Couples rented the rooms by the hour. The managers didn't ban anybody except girls in secondary school uniforms. The love hotels weren't just for the young – old married couples went there to escape their crowded houses. Not for sex, for peace and quiet. The government had to shut the hotels – the prostitutes were taking over.'

Rosa dumped the eggs on a plate and placed it in front of me. I glanced at the counter. No eggs in sight. Guilt grabbed and tugged. Sometimes Rosa and Miguel handed me things (like a tall glass of freshly made orange juice the previous afternoon) and noticing they weren't serving them to anyone else, I realised they were sacrificing for a special guest. I left most of the orange juice untouched; now I claimed I wasn't hungry and couldn't eat the second egg. Rosa slipped it on to a plate and ate it herself.

'Vicente doesn't drink much,' I said. 'And he's too smart to lie down and let a train run over him. Where are you meeting Celia and her daughter?'

'At the photographer's. Parents save up money so their girls can have their pictures done on the day they become women. It's a very important custom. What age do girls become women in Canada?'

I didn't know how to answer. I recalled my mother saying females reaching womanhood in her native Scotland received a house key on their twenty-first birthday. She informed me the same standard applied in the New World, but in my teens I discovered Canadian girls believed that they shed their adolescence when they gained a driving licence at sixteen. In the early stages of the twenty-first century, introduced to sex and drugs and street crime, innumerable twelve- and thirteen-year-olds were undergoing a rite of passage much more scorching than passing a driving test.

'Girls have abortions at fourteen without their parents' permission. I guess they're minors till then. Can I go to the photographer's with you?'

'With us? Sure. Osvaldo will show you his new machine. He carts it from his apartment in the morning and plunks it where customers can't miss seeing it. He's like a father showing off a baby boy.'

Osvaldo's machine was a Gold Star VCR. His flat adjoined his second-floor studio, and as Rosa had predicted, the machine rested in a deliberately visible spot on the first piece of furniture you encountered upon entering the room, a round walnut table. The studio didn't have a television set; presumably, his flat did.

'Ah, you've noticed the movie viewer,' Osvaldo said,

sounding very much like a proud father. 'Gorgeous, isn't it? Two hundred and seventy-six dollars.'

'How did you bring it into the country? There's a one-hundred-dollar ceiling on foreign goods.' I almost blurted out that the last time I flew to Holguín, the medicine alone in my luggage exceeded the customs' limit by $200. What froze my tongue was the memory of Vicente warning me that no one outside the immediate family was to be trusted with information that might interest the authorities.

'I didn't,' Osvaldo replied. 'I bought it in Havana. All very legal. I have the receipt in my apartment.'

'Can you purchase videos in Cuba?'

'There's a dealer in Holguín. He doesn't have many.'

'Hollywood films?'

'Naturally. They're the classiest. He imports movies from Europe. The subtitles are in Spanish. I've got *Forrest Gump*.' He switched to clumsy English and added, '"Chocolates are life. You eat what you eat."'

Osvaldo began speaking and moving quickly, as though he had abruptly realised he was running late and waiting customers crammed the outside corridor. (In point of fact, nobody knocked on his door during the session, and when it ended the corridor was deserted.)

Surveying the profusion of pictures tacked to the walls, I remarked that weddings must be his speciality.

'Weddings, children and passports. I don't do that many passports, perhaps five or six a year. Last week a man stomped in here and threw his photograph at me. "You're the reason my passport application was rejected!" he screamed. "Your picture made me look sinister!" "You're a famous robber and swindler!" I screamed back at him, "You should be congratulating me for capturing your personality!'"

Rosa and I laughed, but Celia was too caught up in her daughter's appearance to grasp the conversation. A wisp of a woman, fortyish and sloe-eyed, she seemed scarcely bigger than the suitcase she had lugged to the studio. The suitcase contained Laura's clothing. Celia escorted her daughter behind a screen and helped her make umpteen changes. Hardly saying a word, Laura obediently struck poses. She sat on a stool, leaned against the window frame, and stood under a wrought-iron lighting fixture pretending to be dreaming of marital joy. Then Osvaldo photographed the girl and her mother wearing similar off-white dresses in front of a painted backdrop of rolling waves and smooth sand, a strange choice since the actual ocean was just over an hour away.

'You know what would be outstanding?' Osvaldo said, gazing at an overstuffed couch of vaguely Victorian styling. 'Laura reclining there in a negligee.'

'Are you serious?' Celia asked.

'Not provocative. Innocent and romantic.'

'We don't have a negligee,' Rosa said.

'I do,' Osvaldo said.

'No,' Celia said firmly. 'I don't need that kind of picture.'

We trooped out of the studio shortly afterwards. Celia and Laura went off somewhere and Rosa and I walked to her house. I commented that Celia didn't smile much. Rosa said life had been mean to Celia. The enduring sorrow she felt over her husband's death from cancer was interwoven with chronic arthritic pain and workplace dissatisfaction. A brilliant administrator, she had been groomed for a top position at a Havana company. Then the Russians swarmed in, permanently freezing her in a mid-level slot. The Russians were as different to Cubans as olive oil was to vodka. The Russians growled commands and drank booze in their offices; Celia's immediate superior was a foul-mouthed sexist. Celia despised them all, and in the twenty years they had worked together, she'd refused to learn a word of Russian. Now she held an executive post in Holguín, still in middle management.

'Osvaldo's sister married a Russian,' Rosa said. 'He dragged her to Leningrad. He was generous to her but the marriage fell apart. He worked all the time and she was lonely and homesick.'

'Photography must be a lucrative profession,' I ventured. 'Two hundred and seventy-six dollars for a VCR.'

'I think a relative in America gave him the money,' she tilted her head and said lightly, 'unless he got it on the black market – selling pictures of fifteen-year-olds in negligees.'

Celia and her daughter lived in a village outside Holguín. The house was a bit of a jolt. I had no clear concept of how a mid-level Cuban executive existed, but I hadn't an inkling it would be this depressingly sparse. There was no glass in the windows (Celia closed the shutters during storms), the walls were bare except for a five-year-old Swiss calendar, and frayed blankets served as room dividers. Four wicker chairs, older than anyone in the room, shared the parlour with a motorcycle smelling of petrol. There were two hotplates in the kitchen, and beyond the kitchen, a dank bathroom with a toilet you flushed by carrying water from a well and filling the tank. Kerosene lamps and candles substituted for electricity. The house was, I thought, another reason for Celia not to smile.

Celia was in the kitchen washing lettuce in a pail. 'You found my place all right,' she said with an expressionless glance. 'Go into the yard. Geraldo was late and we'll be eating in four hours.'

Told that Celia was planning an early dinner, I had skipped lunch. My hunger was certain to expand to discomforting proportions, as would the dilemma of waiting all that time, just hanging around the property: how could we keep the conversation going? We'd be staring at the horizon, blank-brained and mute, wishing the aurora borealis would miraculously appear so we'd have something to say.

I went into the yard. The guests had positioned themselves in a semi-circle facing Geraldo and the pig he was barbecuing over a charcoal pit. Geraldo was somebody's grandfather, and killing and roasting pigs was his forte. He hunched on a stool, slowly turning the dead animal on a pole that entered a gutted and sewn rear end and exited the mouth. The skin had already turned golden-brown; the mixed aroma of charcoal smoke and roasting pork was a gift for the spectators' noses.

Miguel poured me a beer. The government sent couples a free keg on their wedding day and a teetotal bride and groom had donated theirs to Laura's birthday party.

Rosa introduced me to the guests I hadn't met, a bewildering swirl of cousins and nephews, uncles, aunts and family friends. I took a chair in the middle of the semi-circle and looked around. Cacti, weeds and grass grew unhampered amidst palm and mango trees. A pig roamed the distant end of the property, as far as it could get from the pit, and chickens scavenged the ground. A home-made ladder allowed the chickens to roost in a leafy tree overnight, hiding from predators.

'Did you fly here on Cubana?' one of Celia's aunts asked.
'Yes.'

'And you lived to tell the tale? The last time I flew Cubana, the top half of my seat was missing. The stewardess said it was a short trip and I'd be perfectly comfortable as long as I didn't lean back.'

'That beats the Havana train,' said Isabel, a messy-haired artist. 'Twenty hours on an orthopaedic.'

'An orthopaedic?' I queried.

'The seats are so hard that's what we call them.'

'The trains are terrible,' a male cousin offered. 'Hot in the day and cold at night. An old man died sitting across from me. The conductor tossed a blanket over the body and said to pretend it wasn't there. Children were playing hide-and-seek and a little boy crawled under the blanket.'

'Did they sell sandwiches on that trip?' the aunt said. 'The sandwiches are so hard on Cuban trains they could replace the busted seats with them. Edible orthopaedics.'

Everyone was laughing, enjoying the recounting of ghastly experiences they could relate to. Isabel contributed the final train story.

'The sacred cows aren't in India, they're in Cuba,' she told me. 'In this country cows' ears are tattooed with numbers when they are born. If you kill a cow, and you can't prove it was accidental, you get ten years in jail. I was going to Havana and a mile outside of town the train hit a cow. Killed it dead. All of a sudden all these people started showing up. Some were running and some were riding bicycles. Some had axes and some had big knives. By the time the police got there, all that was left of the cow was the head with the tattooed ears. They even ran off with the tail.'

I heard a car horn beep three times. José was signalling his arrival in the Chevy. He parked beside the road and sauntered through the house into the yard. He was the pleased possessor of two bottles of Havana Club. Glasses were filled, Celia summoned from the kitchen. José proposed a toast to Laura. The demure recipient of the toast made a quiet-voiced request.

'Absolutely not,' was her mother's stern response. 'You're too young to drink.'

'When will you feel I'm old enough?'

'Some day, but not fifteen.'

'Sixteen?'

'I haven't decided. Sixteen, seventeen, eighteen. Sometime before you're twenty.'

Celia watched the pig roasting for a while and then returned to the house. When she vanished from sight, Isabel handed Laura her glass. 'Don't tell your mother I did this. In my family, fifteen's the customary age for drinking your first rum – and smoking your first cigarette.'

Laura sipped the rum and then handed the glass back. 'That tastes nice,' she said. 'I don't want a cigarette. Now or ever.'

'How about a cigar?' Miguel teased. 'Unless you're secretly smoking them already.'

A relative prodded Isabel to repeat her train story for José. When she was finished, he laughed and said, 'You know Gustavo Pérez? He has a farm between Baguanos and Banes. This awful noise woke him up in the middle of the night. It sounded like an animal suffering great pain. He hurled himself to his feet and raced into the yard. He saw a stranger dart out of the cowshed and into the bush. Gustavo went into the shed. His cow was in agony. The man had taken a knife and cut a piece of beef out of its side.'

José swallowed the rest of his drink in a fast gulp and then went to the car to retrieve Laura's present, a cotton V-neck sweater. Most of the gifts were clothing or sweets. Isabel's offering was a compact mirror and a lipstick, which she said, she'd persuade Celia to let Laura wear.

'Where's that boy of ours?' Rosa asked Miguel. 'He should've been here long ago. Did the motorbike drop dead?'

Miguel shrugged and unscrewed the second bottle of rum.

The motorcycle hadn't dropped dead. Vicente crept down the road, dodging potholes as though they were the open jaws of rabid dogs. The cake he was afraid of jarring and wrecking rested in a topless cardboard box in the sidecar.

'Sorry I'm late,' he said, carting the box into the yard. 'I drove slow all the way.'

'Three hours in this heat?' his mother said. 'The cake's melted.'

'No, mother, it's OK. I stopped to see Nena after I picked it up. She stashed it in the refrigerator.'

'And there wasn't a blackout?'

'No, mother, there wasn't a blackout.'

For their child's fifteenth birthday celebration, parents received a meringue marvel. The boys' cakes were blue and white, the girls' pink and white. Parents applied to the government for the subsidised dessert months in advance and were obligated to supply something the baker could construct the cake upon, a metal baking tray, a wooden chair seat, anything flat and sturdy.

Laura's pink and white cake was deposited in the centre

of the long table set up in the yard. Laura, Celia and the guests were awed by the meringue circles and squiggles and the happy birthday inscription, *Feliz Cumpleaños*. Celia said Canadians ate cake every Sunday and therefore it wasn't as exciting an event for me as it was for them. Vicente said the baker was luckier than anyone in Canada – he ate cake three times a day.

Twilight softened the air and then, around eight o'clock, we were in darkness. I should have known better than to fret about a group of Cubans running out of conversation. They talked around the pit, they talked during the candlelit dinner under a mango tree. They were talking as I crossed the yard at midnight and passed Laura sleeping on a porch cot. She was fifteen, a woman, but childhood hadn't freed her yet. She was cuddling a rag doll.

chapter seventeen

Miguel was a bureaucrat, and like fellow members of the clan, he was a choice candidate for the scorn and ridicule of frustrated and enraged citizens. I tried to imagine him shuffling papers, wielding a rubber stamp and rudely dismissing the common folk coming cap in hand to his desk, but the impression wouldn't stick. He was too cordial, too prone to laughter, and, perhaps naively, I held the opinion that anyone writing sensitive poetry exploring the joy and pain of human existence couldn't be an uncompassionate son of a bitch at the office.

His occupation was, he admitted, unforgivingly mundane. The worst part of it was being under the supervision of a person of minor intelligence who thought the work was enthralling. Whenever an internal report was finished ahead of schedule or a consignment of hard-to-get office supplies arrived, the man bounded from his seat, enthusiastically rubbed his hands together and exclaimed, 'Marvellous, marvellous! This is truly good news!'

Why didn't Miguel resign? With his experience he was certain to garner a satisfying position elsewhere. When I broached that question over coffee in his Holguín house, he replied, 'I'm not going anywhere. My job's boring, but I'm proud to be contributing to my country's welfare. The bureaucratic wheels turn slowly, but they do turn. I'm

Cuba's servant. Efficient and loyal until they wrap my coffin in the Cuban flag and lower it into the ground.'

For Cubans, patriotism wasn't a matter of hauling yourself begrudgingly to your feet when the national anthem preceded a sporting event, nor was it an excuse for business-orchestrated campaigns urging consumers to pick indigenous products over foreign imports. Cuban nationalism was intensely emotional: it burned in the blood. Schoolroom mantras to patriotism implanted it there and the national anthem, '*Morir por la Patria es Vivir*' ('To Die for the Fatherland is to Live') helped stretch its longevity. To most Cubans, country meant Communism and Communism meant country. Miguel was no exception but his allegiance to that concept wasn't born and nurtured in classrooms. It grew out of the arid soil of a haunting childhood incident.

I had a faint knowledge of Miguel's background – affluent merchant's son, university student, soldier – until the afternoon in 1993 when he filled in the blanks. I had made a date to meet him at the public beach north of Holguín, a short walk from my oceanfront hotel. The sun was high and white, the ocean a silvery glint. Guardalavaca Beach, a strip of white sand, lay between the quiet Atlantic and a lovely grove of large, leafy, wind-twisted trees. Holguín artists sold crafts and lithograph prints under the trees, and older Cubans, dressed in street clothes, sat gazing at the swimmers as though they were Tropicana entertainers staging a show. Miguel and I took cold drinks from a beach bar and nestled beneath an almond tree. He was in a reflective mood, in no hurry to reclaim his desk in the city.

He asked what my youthful impressions had been of his country. Carmen Miranda, I said, swaying and singing to salsa music in a film called *Havana Week-end*. (I learned in future years that she wasn't Cuban and the film was shot on Hollywood sets.) The palm tree on the stamp a millionaire gave me, the Havana Sugar Kings playing in the International League. César Romero marketing charm, Ricky Ricardo yelling at Lucy, a fetchingly decorated cigar box in a Victoria smoke shop window, the label on a discarded Bacardi bottle I found in a field. Blue skies and exotic women. What were his early impressions of Canada? Snow and bears, he said, and the entire population of a few thousand people shivering in log cabins.

'Did you have a happy childhood?'

Not really, I confessed. My father was an alcoholic, my mother a malicious critic of his and everyone else's conduct. They slept in separate rooms and seldom went anywhere together. Love was a word I couldn't recall either of them uttering. When our next-door neighbour was affectionate, kissing her child, my mother rebuked her, saying too much attention spoiled children. Our oak and mahogany dining room was as joyless as a dental lab to me. I detested the lengthy silences, the standing rule that each scrap of food must be eaten, the black leather belt beside my father's plate that was a menacing reminder of the penalty for rebellious conduct. In that room, I developed a life-long abhorrence for floral-patterned tea cups – my seat at the square, oak table faced the sideboard exhibiting my mother's costly collection.

'How sad,' Miguel said. 'My parents were good to me and my brother. My father did strike Luis once, for starting a grass fire at our second house in the country. My mother was constantly praising us, buying us toys and sweet cakes.

Our family was full of love and affection, but it wasn't free of strife. No, not at all.'

The family's country house was actually a working farm in Oriente province. A peasant family domiciled in a tin-roof shack on the property helped harvest the fruit crop and raised corn on a small plot behind their shack, half of which they were obliged to surrender to Miguel's father. When the family bought a pregnant goat and it bore two kids, his father automatically received one of them. Miguel grew up feeling sorry for the peasants. There was no running water and no electricity in the earth-floor dwelling. Their children were shoeless and scabby and dressed in filthy clothing. Don't shed tears for them, his father said. They are glad to have a roof over their head and food in their stomachs.

In the late 1950s Miguel and his family were holidaying at the country house. His father was awakened during the night by distant voices. He lit a lamp and the talking ceased. He peered outside, and seeing nothing, returned to bed. The next morning Batista soldiers came to the house. Castro rebels had attacked an army post and the soldiers demanded to know which direction they had gone in. Miguel's father admitted hearing them, but it was windy and the voices could've come from anywhere. The sergeant in charge of the soldiers accused him of lying to protect the rebels. He drew his revolver and marched Miguel's father out of the house and into a palm grove. The family huddled in the yard, petrified and powerless. They heard a gunshot. Miguel's mother was hysterical. She ran into the grove, Miguel and his brother close on her heels. His father sat on the ground, holding his hand to his chest. There was blood on his shirt and he was in a state of shock. The soldiers had ordered him to kneel and place his right hand on a tree stump. The sergeant fired a bullet through it.

'We wrapped his hand in a shirt and drove to Santiago. The doctor treating the wound said my father was fortunate the soldiers hadn't killed him; that they'd killed other Castro supporters for protecting rebels. My father protested that he wasn't a Castro supporter, he was a prosperous merchant without a drop of political blood in his body. He went to the army barracks to have the sergeant charged. An officer listened to his account and said, "You're the person we should charge. If I hear the slightest whisper about you protecting rebels again, you'll be in deep trouble. The hand wound was a warning." At our home in Santiago, my mother changed the dressings but the wound got infected. Gangrene set in and his arm had to be amputated below the elbow.'

His business came apart at the seams. Clients transferred their trade to other merchants because they were wary of associating with a rumoured rebel sympathiser. But most of the things that happened were plain bad luck. Investments failed, the country house burned to the ground, his wealthy silent partner perished in a freak boating accident. Within a year of the shooting, Miguel's father was bankrupt. Reluctantly, the family packed its belongings – French provincial furniture, English china, the pink Art Deco clock that Miguel still owned – and moved to a Havana tenement. His father gained employment as a night watchman, his mother cleaned houses and government offices.

And then, on New Year's Eve, 1959, Cuba entered a radical new era, becoming the first Marxist-Leninist nation in the western hemisphere. Batista and his closest henchmen scampered from a party at the Presidential Palace, and their wives and daughters, wearing ball gowns, boarded an aircraft transporting them into exile. The populace craved retribution for the injustice and corruption that had characterised the dethroned regime: Castro, a genius at deducing and fulfilling public desires, established special courts in major centres to try Batista stooges accused of committing criminal deeds. A trial staged in a Havana sports stadium was televised and, gathering in a barrio courtyard, Miguel's family witnessed the event with their neighbours.

'Jesús Sosa Blanco was among the prisoners. He was an army major known to have tortured and murdered dozens of people at the Santiago garrison. My father cursed him throughout the trial and cheered the reading of the death verdict. There were five hundred executions and thousands of soldiers were jailed all over Cuba. My father was confident the sergeant who shot him was brought to justice. Not for shooting him, of course. He reasoned that a person that vicious must've done more atrocious things to others.'

Losing his arm and his affluent lifestyle turned Miguel's father bitter and moody. The Revolution had no special significance for him. It was, however, of great value to his sons. Both completed their schooling and compulsory military service, and owing to their superb academic records, were granted free university education.

In 1973 his father died of a heart attack. Going through his clothing, Miguel's mother discovered a crumpled snapshot of a young woman seated on a doorstep. Someone had written her name and address on the back. His mother summoned Miguel and said she desperately needed to know the truth – was this woman his father's lover? She begged him to talk to the woman.

'My father was infirm and grouchy and hadn't much money. Not the sort of old man young women are apt to be attracted to. So maybe he was stealing stuff where he worked and using the money to pay her for sex. Or my mother had it wrong, and he and the young woman were merely friends.'

He went to the address on the photograph. It was a shop selling government books. He asked to speak to the woman, but the clerk at the cash desk said she was running an errand.

'I can't wait,' Miguel said. 'Do you happen to know her home address? This is a personal affair.'

'No, I don't,' the clerk said. 'Her husband's waiting for her. You can ask him.'

The clerk motioned towards the rear of the shop. Miguel instantly recognised the man leafing through a manual; he was the sergeant who had shot his father. Stunned and confused, Miguel ran outside. He walked for miles before hopping on a bus.

'How did he find the sergeant? Where did he acquire the picture? Was he planning to harm the woman to even the score with her husband? I never saw my father as a violent person, but there were many, many Cubans whose friends and families swore they were non-violent people – and they murdered for Batista. Was my father like that? Did he vanish all those times because he was stalking the sergeant and his young wife? I'll never know the answer. Never.'

Miguel tore up the photograph and steered clear of the bookshop. He was frightened by his own powerful inclination to avenge his father by trailing the woman home and hacking her husband's arm with a machete. When the opportunity arose to fill a vacant bureaucratic post in Holguín, he grabbed it.

'Thank goodness I did. I came to understand that the best method of dealing with the ugliness of the past was to stick it behind me. I resolved to do what I could to keep vicious animals like Batista and the sergeant who shot my father devoid of political power. We must continue to build a strong Cuba. So strong that when El Jefe dies, the Communist system won't die with him. The Miami worms and the CIA have selected the government they'd like to rule us and it is our task, the true Cubans, to keep them on the American side of the water.'

The perceived threat of an American invasion to install a Miami-formed government inspired the formation of the Territorial Troops Militia in the 1980s. Now more than one million volunteers engage in periodic military training each year; guerrilla warfare, which the Castro rebels had won their stripes at, was a primary component.

We left our glasses at the beach bar and walked to the bus station. We passed a group of tourists wearing green palm-leaf hats, a trucker staring despairingly at his vehicle's two flat tyres. Miguel said three years of army service had taught him how to handle himself and the idea of defending Cuba in armed combat failed to unnerve him.

'You know what unnerves me? The nightmares I've been having since I was a youngster. I'm haunted by the day the Batista soldiers came to our house and my father was shot. Every now and then, I picture it in my sleep, the shooting and the amputation, and I wake up sweating. If I'd attacked the sergeant in Havana, the dreams might've stopped. Rosa says that's nonsense but she's no psychiatrist.' He coiled an arm around my shoulder and said humorously, 'This will be my retirement project. I'll have nothing else to do, I'll track the sergeant down. He'll be old and depending on a cane. I'll take a machete, hack the cane to shreds, and we'll see whether or not Rosa's right.'

chapter eighteen

'When the full moon rises
I will go to Santiago de Cuba
The roofs of palm will sing
I will go to Santiago …
I will go to Santiago …'

Federico García Lorca wrote those lines on a warm summer's day in 1930. He was visiting Havana, and entranced by the capital's hedonistic atmosphere, he almost didn't get to the far end of the island and the city that lit his imagination. Fresh from Laura's birthday fête, I journeyed to Santiago for many of the same motives the Spanish poet did. The country's second largest city, the prominent characteristics setting it apart from other Cuban centres included Haitian-influenced food, music and Santería ceremonies. Until the introduction of train travel, trade between Santiago and Hispaniola, the island shared by Haiti and the Dominican Republic, was extensive. Havana, 600 miles west, was a distant whimper compared to the robust voice of Hispaniola, a 200-mile boat ride over the Windward Passage. French-speaking Haitian slaves found refuge in Santiago, leading to a fascinating mix of cultural ideas. Haitian dishes blended with Cuban on meal tables, local rumba bands acquired a Haitian sound, and some Santería practitioners staged secret rites containing procedures gleaned from Haitian voodoo.

When Lorca visited Santiago, the Bacardís ruled the social roost. The family had been producing premier-class rum since the 1860s, and a seat at a Bacardí dinner party was greatly cherished: one nouveau riche merchant framed the invitation card he received and exhibited it on his desk. Castro's decision to expropriate the family business caused the Bacardís to quit the country in 1960 and build a mammoth plant in Puerto Rico. To avert a copyright conflict in international courts, the Castro government renamed the old Bacardí product Havana Club. Miguel had said I could purchase a bottle of 25-year-old Havana Club at the Santiago distillery for $10. As I had never consumed rum that ancient, I went to the factory on Jesús Menéndez, a street facing the city's main railway tracks. The skeletal frame of an unfinished terminal building – construction started a decade earlier – loomed like a huge beast stripped of all flesh.

The distillery was the oldest rum-making facility in Cuba, and owing to the Bacardís' affluence and superb personal taste, I imagined a colonial delight, stone and marble, columns, frescoes and towers. It failed to cross my mind that regardless of the family's wealth and refinement, the factory was, after all, just a factory and businessmen aren't inclined to prize splendour above economy and efficiency when commissioning industrial premises. With the exception of two world globes above the entrance – both painted a fading red – the Havana Club building was plain and cheerless.

Busloads of Canadian and German tourists filled the sales room. A Cubanacán guide warned that photographs were forbidden and no one was permitted to tour the distillery due to security concerns.

'Whaddya think we'll do?' a Canadian man protested. 'Pinch your recipe?'

'Yeah, we'll pinch it,' another man chimed in. 'We'll go to the hotel and brew it in the bathtub.'

I squeezed through the crowd to the counter. The clerk was out of 15, 20 and 25-year-old rum. The best he could supply was the seven-year-old variety that was sold in every tourist gift shop. Disappointed, I reached for a glass of free three-year-old that a tour guide was distributing. The glass was dirty.

'Don't get your shorts in a knot,' a white-haired woman advised me. 'The alcohol will kill the germs.'

I swallowed the booze and went outside. In recognition of its citizens' brave spirit, Santiago was the only Cuban centre awarded the official title '*Ciudad Heroe*' (Hero City). Santiago natives had distinguished themselves during nineteenth-century independence uprisings and the Castro-led insurrection. I took a taxi to Moncada barracks, the site of the ill-fated 1953 attack. The Batista army post had been converted into a public school and a museum displaying guerrilla fatigues, weapons and various paraphernalia contributed by Castro soldiers. Students attending the school didn't have to enter the museum to be reminded of the battle that had occurred on the grounds: bullet holes in the exterior walls had gone unrepaired.

Revolution, a Cuban adventurer told Laurie Lee, was part and parcel of the country's national psyche. In his 1969 autobiographical book, *As I Walked Out One Midsummer Morning*, Lee recalled running into a silk-shirted dandy in a Cadiz bar during the Spanish Civil War. 'I am Cuban,' the stranger proclaimed. 'We are very wild kind of men. All we are interested in is dames and revolutions …'

The silk-shirted dandy was not, I had long ago ascertained, truly representative of the average Cuban male. They weren't all wild men and they weren't solely interested in dames and revolution. Yet Laurie Lee's Cuban leapt to mind after I departed Moncada and went downtown. Cobbled streets spoked out from Parque Céspedes, a large square across from a historic cathedral (built in 1523), a historic house (construction started in 1513) and a historic city hall (Castro stood on the balcony to address the joyous masses when his forces captured Santiago). Weary and hot, I dropped onto an unhistoric park bench and devoured lunch, a melting Mars bar. The brawny youth next to me was reading a collection of José Martí quotations.

'José Martí,' I said. 'A great person.'

The youth glanced up. 'Yes,' he nodded.

I wiped my chocolate-smeared hands on my jeans. Cubans in the square noting the action would've been appalled. Jeans were too highly regarded to wilfully commit an offence against them.

The youth closed the book, appraised my face and said, 'Where are you from?'

I nearly fled. That was the universal opening move for street hustlers. Whatever you answered – New York, Madrid, Blackpool – they invariably replied, 'I've heard it's a beautiful place.'

The youth wasn't a hustler. He was an athlete. And he hadn't been reading the book; he was memorising favourite passages.

'I really don't understand why Martí is so significant to Cubans,' I said. 'It must go beyond his martyrdom. This country's had countless martyrs. The Santiago airport – Frank País – is named after a student who lost his life fighting Batista.'

'Yes, it goes beyond just martyrdom. But you aren't Cuban and you can't understand. The fact is, the less *Norte Americanos* know about our heroes, the better. Your people have a history of taking things that are precious to a nation and exploiting them. You know 'Guantanamera'? Hotel bands play it. Tourists dance and guzzle rum and hum along as though it were a silly love song. Can you tell me the name of the composer of 'Guantanamera'?'

'An American folksinger. Pete Seeger.' He wrote it, I recollected, but it was a sixties group, The Sandpipers, that rocketed it onto what was then called the *Hit Parade*.

'Your Pete Seeger was an exploiter. He was excited by dollar signs. He wrote the pretty melody, but a patriot who disdained money wrote the poignant words – José Martí.'

I tried to think of the lyrics. They involved, I foggily remembered, somebody pining for a woman. 'Pete Seeger's a life-long leftist. He wouldn't be excited by dollar signs.'

The youth's expression reflected his desire for an argument, but politics being a treacherous swamp, he hurled himself onto safer ground. The conga dance originated in Oriente province, he said. The world's tiniest bird, a bee-sized hummingbird, existed in Matanzas. Santiago was famous for Pru, a soft drink blending vanilla, pepper leaves, pine needles, soapberries and India root. 'A *Norte Americano* will come here and steal the formula. You'll be ordering Pru-Cola with your Big Mac.' Observing a pair of uniformed cops checking a young woman's ID card, he plunged into the swamp. 'Those people are evil,' he spat.

'The police have their bad elements. It's the same everywhere. We have bad cops in Canada too.'

'The police step on us and tread lightly past the biggest enemies of the state. There are Communists smuggling drugs and driving new cars and entertaining their mistresses at Varadero Beach. Not El Comandante, but the big shots surrounding him. El Comandante is honest, he has compassion. I shiver thinking of the day he dies and his brother is in control. Raúl has no feeling. Raúl's heart is a slab of marble.'

Without a free press to convey character impressions, it was amazing how effectively word-of-mouth descriptions spread to the nation's furthest corners, blackening or polishing reputations. The 75-year-old Fidel was considered to be a flamboyant, loquacious charmer, a grandfatherly figure who, turning up unexpectedly at ball games, factories and town squares, thrived upon hugging and kissing everyone in his path. At seventy, Raúl was said to be a hard, moody, arrogant individual who loathed mingling with the masses.

Was Raúl's negative image bang-on accurate? Maybe, maybe not. The absence of analytical journalism in Cuba and Raúl's abhorrence of foreign press interviews rendered a definite conclusion impossible. There was, however, no denying that while Fidel was frequently branded ruthless by the international media, particularly in the United States, his lesser-known younger brother actually swung a heavier fist.

The fifth of the Castro clan's seven children, Raúl had studied at Jesuit colleges in Santiago and Havana, and at the University of Havana. A member of the Juventud Socialista (Socialist Youth) organisation, he had visited several Iron Curtain countries in 1953, and upon his return to Cuba he was at Fidel's side during the Moncada raid. Released from prison in the 1955 general amnesty, he pledged to match Batista 'terror for terror', ordering the 'elimination by gunshot' of the dictator's henchmen. Fidel approved the edict, but the brothers did not always see eye to eye on other matters. Fidel was against kidnapping foreigners, yet Raúl abducted fifty Canadians and Americans in 1958 (Batista met his demands and the hostages were freed).

Then there was the Morales incident. Escaping to Mexico after the authorities claimed he had planted a bomb in a cinema, Raúl instructed the exiled guerrillas under his command to march thirteen miles a day to stay fit. A former teacher, Calixto Morales Hernández, said the marches were pointless and he refused to participate. At his court martial, Raúl advocated the death penalty. Fidel was more lenient. He recommended expelling Morales from the rebel army, which the jury subsequently decided to do. Writing of the episode later, guerrilla leader Alberto Bayo noted: 'Fidel is flexible, Raúl is tempered steel. Fidel is more reachable, Raúl is a calculating machine.'

Raúl's machine-like demeanour was evident again in 1989 when one of his closest friends, General Arnaldo Ochoa Sánchez, was charged with corruption. Raúl thoroughly denounced him in court. Six months after Fidel praised Ochoa as 'an exceptional warrior of the fatherland' for his service in Angola and Ethiopia, the general was executed. Numerous Cuba-watchers opined that the cocaine smuggling and 'dissipation' accusations were invented to rid the brothers of a public figure whose popularity threatened to equal Fidel's.

The global rumour mill spun out reports that Fidel was well aware that the people disliked Raúl, and was thinking of alternative successors, notably National Assembly president Ricardo Alarcon de Quesada. But everyone I ever discussed the topic with predicted that Raúl, the head of the armed forces and the No. 2 man in the Party hierarchy, had waited so long in the wings that Fidel was bound to anoint him. Fidel hadn't kept the Communist torch burning – outlasting seven American presidents – by being predictable, yet in 2001 he did exactly what my Cuban friends said he'd do: he announced that his brother would succeed him someday.

'Raúl may not be that awful,' I said. 'He's done good things lately.'

The youth's eyebrows lifted. 'Really? And what are they?'

'He pushed for the free-enterprise farmers' markets. He was the driving force behind the plan to send military officers to run hotels and factories, which should improve their efficiency and be a big help to the general economy. A friend of mine said Raúl has been going to different cities, giving speeches, overcoming his aversion to public gatherings. In Holguín, his message was, Cuba needs more food, not more rhetoric and guns.'

'Propaganda. The Communists are attempting to fool us into thinking like you do – Raúl may not be that awful. They don't want riots in the streets. Well, there will be riots – and deaths. Cubans won't be governed by a ruthless autocrat. We're born with this gene in our system that sleeps until we're stuck beneath the boot of somebody we hate. Then the gene wakes up screaming, "Revolution! Revolution!" There are weapons in the Sierra Maestra. Smuggled weapons from Florida, rifles stolen from Cuban military camps. There will be revolution, señor. I swear it. With Raúl Castro as El Comandante, revolution is inevitable.'

chapter nineteen

The road to El Cobre ran through the foothills of the Sierra Maestra. The taxi passed slopes densely covered with trees and underbrush. I pictured myself domiciled deep within the mountains, a valiant member of Castro's ragtag guerrilla band. It was an image I couldn't sustain: sleeping on miserably hard ground, eating beans and rice, slapping mosquitoes, stomping on scorpions and evading troops yearning to kill you was an unappealing vision for a *Norte Americano* inclined to feel abused when a thunderstorm wiped cable off his TV screen. Were there weapons hidden out there? Was a new generation of firebrands primed for revolution? The Santiago youth's claims were likely hollow bravado, a spur-of-the-moment invention to impress a gullible foreigner. Then again, when a Batista informer at the University of Havana overheard a law student named Castro speak of going into the mountains someday and turning the tide of Cuban history, he attributed it to empty boasting.

Twelve miles outside Santiago, I rode through El Cobre, a dusty town where, in the 1500s, slaves had laboured at Latin America's first open copper mine. The church that drew me to the Sierra Maestra controlled a hilltop two miles beyond the town. The steep green uninhabited slope rising behind the domed whitewashed building seemed purposely built in that location to furnish a dramatic effect. On the road between the town and the church the taxi passed tall stalks of butterfly jasmine. The snow-white flowers had a fabled role in the War of Independence. Females sympathising with the Martí-quoting insurgents wove butterfly-jasmine flowers into their hair.

El Cobre was the Lourdes of Cuba. It was added to the Vatican's nonpareil collection of miracle sites in the seventeenth century. Two brothers, Juan and Rodrigo de Hoyos, and a ten-year-old slave, Juan Moreno, were sailing a small boat in the Bay of Nipe when they spotted a statue, standing upright, on a smooth-planed board. Hauling the foot-high statue out of the water, they discovered it was a wooden representation of a mulatta Virgin Mary. An inscription on the board read, '*Yo soy la Virgen de la Caridad*' ('I am the Virgin of Charity').

The brothers installed the statue in a thatched shrine on the road to El Cobre. On three successive nights the mulatta Virgin vanished; it was found the following mornings on a hill closer to town. The legend surrounding the statue's mysterious nocturnal travelling was augmented by stories concerning miraculous cures. The statue was transferred to an El Cobre chapel, and when a new church was erected in the 1920s, it was situated near the main altar. Curiously, Ernest Hemingway's Nobel Prize medal had been assigned a display case at the church. He pocketed the Stockholm cash and dedicated the medal to the Virgin. The medal was stolen in 1988 and when the police recovered it, the church locked it up in a bank vault.

The taxi driver said I was fortunate not to be there during a mass pilgrimage. Thousands of people descended upon El Cobre, clogging the road with cars, bicycles and horse carts, and lining up to shuffle past the statue. Most of the pilgrims prayed for miracles to banish ill health or emotional problems. I had nothing to pray for. Actually, that wasn't true. I was in my fifth year of suffering from tinnitus, an endless ringing in the ears, and there were unpleasant blotches on my character I'd have loved to shed, among them a mean-spirited habit of cheering and thanking the gods whenever a certain novelist whose money pile was substantially larger than mine received a wretched review. But I'd been to religious shrines in Mexico, Europe and Quebec and none of them emitted healing vibrations potent enough to put me on my knees.

El Cobre didn't either.

An ageing woman was standing at the altar, head bent and arms outstretched as though she was nailed to a cross. Close by, another woman, also on the dark side of sixty, was kneeling and silently moving her lips. The third worshipper in the church, a man in his late thirties, deposited something on the shrine under the Virgin Mary statue. Walking towards the entrance, he limped. I approached the shrine. Encased in glass, the statue's permanent home was a wall alcove behind the main altar. Wrapped in a gold and copper cape, the Virgin Mary cradled the baby Jesus.

In the Chapel of Miracles behind the statue, I looked at the objects worshippers had laid on an altar. There were bouquets of newly cut bougainvillea, unusual stones, a lizard brooch, an ancient silver coin, locks of hair, bronzed baby shoes, a wristwatch and a dead bird wrapped in pink ribbon. Apart from those items, there was no evidence in the church that the mulatta Mary was a dual-purpose figure; to the Santería faithful, she was the goddess Oshún.

The cross-hanging woman issued a loud gasping noise.

Her kneeling companion looked up and hissed, 'Stop that. You're mocking the Saviour.'

The woman collapsed her arms. 'I wasn't mocking Him. I was praying.'

'Pray like other people do, or come by yourself next time.'

'I'm sorry. I won't do it again.' Setting eyes on me, the woman arranged her face in a disapproving frown. Sightseers were not welcome at El Cobre. In 1993 a group of tourists were advised not to enter the shrine while a service was being conducted. The tourists barged into the church, tongues and video cameras rolling, and a scuffle broke out. The police had to be summoned and now the locals regarded foreigners as disrespectful louts.

I went outside. A squat, bespectacled priest was slowly pacing the landing at the top of the broad stairway leading up to the building. He was smoking an ugly smelling cigarette.

'There's a dead bird on the shrine,' I said.

'Yes, I know,' he said. 'I'll remove it shortly.'

'Is that a common practice among Santería followers – offering dead birds?'

'No, not common. To my knowledge, we haven't had one here before. We've had a dead rooster, and someone donated a glass of animal blood. At least, we assumed it was animal blood.'

'What other unique objects have you had?'

'Why do you want to know?'

'No special reason.'

'We had a landmine. Not the whole mine, just pieces of it. The soldier offering it was in Angola and he wasn't injured in the explosion. Apparently his friends were blown up and killed. He wrote a note and attached it to the offering. We wouldn't have known he was with the Cuban army in Angola if he hadn't done that. We don't question why people leave things at the shrine. Our policy is not to make a fuss. To be respectful.'

'What did the note say?'

He furrowed his forehead and regarded me suspiciously. I thought he was going to ask me why I was interested in knowing that. 'The soldier's note?' he replied after a pause. '"Thank you." That's all it said. He wasn't thanking us, he was thanking the Virgin.'

'There are stories that Fidel Castro believes in Santería. That he wrapped a goddess's statue in combat clothing before starting the Revolution.'

'Here. They say it was here. I haven't come across anyone who saw him do it. There's a Fidel Castro figurine in the chapel. You may have seen it. It shows him in an army uniform. It was donated by his mother. She was a good woman, a good Catholic. Some people could have mistaken the figurine for the statue Fidel Castro supposedly brought for a Santería offering.'

'Santería's growing. More followers each year.'

'So they say. But don't think for a moment that Santería's growth means Catholicism's death. The Romans failed to destroy us, and the Red Chinese, and no matter how big Santería is, our religion will be bigger.' He took a final drag, and grinding the cigarette under his shoe, said, 'I must go. Have a lovely day.'

chapter twenty

The Carretera Central Highway held the country together, twisting up the middle of the island like a deformed spine. Cruising north on the highway, the air conditioning in the rented Nissan was cranked up so high it should have frosted the windows. I passed transport trucks, timeless cars and smoky, rattling buses that looked as though they had scarcely half-a-mile's life remaining in them. Mountains rose and shrank, agricultural land imposed obedience upon jungle confusion.

Santiago lay far behind, Havana far ahead.

Shortly after two o'clock, I grew hungry and turned off the highway on to a dirt road rimmed by coconut palms. I was after a peaceful spot where I could stretch my legs and eat the sandwich I'd bought in Santiago. I thought I had the road all to myself. A mile or so from the highway, I sighted a down-at-the-heel pickup truck parked in the centre of the road. The driver was kneeling over a prostrate female body. He straightened and gestured for me to stop. I pulled over and alighted.

'What happened?'

The driver was unshaven and moon-faced. His breath smelled of alcohol.

'An accident. She's knocked out. Take her to the clinic.'

'What clinic?'

'The Family Doctor Clinic.'

'Where is it?'

He pointed up the road. 'The village.'

The girl was fifteen or sixteen; she was chunky and bow-mouthed, and a polka-dot bandanna circled her head. For a moment, I thought she was dead, but as I knelt to check her breathing, she began to regain consciousness. Like an actor in a television drama, I said with false authority, 'You're going to be all right.'

The driver grabbed a bicycle lying between the girl and the truck and heaved it onto the pickup. 'Go to the clinic,' he said. 'The doctor'll fix her.'

He climbed into the truck and sped off towards the highway, raising dust and doubts about his concern for the girl's health. The girl struggled into a sitting position.

'I'm OK,' she said weakly. 'I don't think anything's broken.'

'What happened?'

'The truck hit me.' Clutching my hand, she pulled herself erect. 'Where's the bicycle?'

'The driver took it.'

'Oh, no. My sister will scream. It's her bike.'

'I'm sorry. I should've realised he was stealing it.' There was a lump on her forehead and a bleeding cut on her cheek. 'I'll take you to the village. A doctor should examine you.'

The Family Doctor Clinic was at the end of the main street. Villagers and city volunteers had combined forces to build a long low building next to a creek. The doctor resided in the rear, a kitchen window awarding him a calming perspective of grazing horses and banana groves. In the waiting room, half a dozen men and women wearing worn *campesino* clothing hunched on rough wooden benches. They had the collective look of hard-luck people accustomed to waiting. The nurse was a semi-blonde. I lacked the courage to ask whether she had bungled the dyeing process or if she had deliberately left patches of her hair midnight black. I explained that I was going to Havana and wouldn't be there when the police arrived from a nearby town.

'That's not good,' she said disapprovingly. 'The police will want details. I'll have Dr Sánchez see you. He can write a report for the police.' She piloted the girl down a bare corridor. 'You poor creature,' she said. 'You got a terrible fright. The man hitting you deserves to be shot.'

'I can't stay long,' I said to the nurse's back. 'I have to find a hotel for the night.'

I plopped onto a bench. The patients stared. I reckoned I was the first foreigner they'd seen in the village in decades, if not since Queen Isabella's hirelings explored the region. I silently hoped no one outside was helping themselves to a commemorative souvenir of The Day The Foreigner Came To Our Village, a Nissan steering wheel. When the girl reappeared, her cheek was bandaged.

'The doctor says I'm not seriously hurt,' she said. 'I'm to report any dizziness, or a bad headache.' She touched the lump on her forehead. 'He said this will yellow and the swelling will go away.'

The nurse sent me to the inner office.

'Good afternoon,' Dr Sánchez said cordially. 'You're a rare bird. We don't get foreigners in our community. What part of America are you from?'

'I'm not from America,' I said righteously, as if I was being accused of war crimes. 'I'm Canadian.'

'Excuse me, I forget they're separate countries. I don't know why I forget. My father is in Montreal.' He scribbled a few notes regarding the accident. 'A green truck with a black box and two missing headlights. The police will locate the scoundrel, you can be sure of that.' He rubbed his neck and drew himself up from a squeaky swivel chair covered by a ripped cushion. He was big; bullish shoulders, wrists he'd have trouble fitting a watch around. 'I need a rest. A bite to eat. When my nurse said you were foreign, I thought you might do me a little favour. I understand you're in a hurry. I'll be quick.'

In the corridor, I remarked that although the United States placed travel limits on its citizens, there seemed to be plenty of them in Cuba. And not just ex-Cubans visiting relatives.

'Businessmen,' the doctor said. 'There's money to be earned and people circumvent the law. You run across Americans on flights between Havana and Nassau. Cuban Customs is exceptionally friendly. Passports go unmarked. Entry and exit data is stamped on a separate sheet of paper. American Customs don't know the businessmen were here.'

'Brilliant.'

The Ministry of Health official decorating the clinic hadn't taken Dr Sánchez's dimensions into account, and consequently the bed in the living quarters was short and narrow. The doctor slept with his feet hanging over the end and twice he had been abruptly awakened when he rolled off and hit the concrete floor. The most appreciated object in the utilitarian kitchen was the refrigerator. It was eighteen months old and manufactured in Moscow. Dr Sánchez had dubbed the shiny white box Anna Karenina.

'As a young man, I adored that lady,' he said. 'The refrigerator will die – Soviet products tend to go to a premature grave – and I'll tell everyone it threw itself onto the railway tracks.'

Dr Sánchez had been dispatched to the village as a voluntary member of the Family Doctor programme. Detecting signs of erosion in the healthcare system, the government launched a national project in 1985 entailing the posting of hundreds of physicians to urban and rural clinics. Each physician was responsible for 120 families. Preventative medicine was a priority. Aided by the Family Doctor programme, the Ministry of Health had repaired the cracks in the system. Cuba's medical standards in the 1980s impressed the world. A widely acknowledged barometer for appraising a nation's healthcare status, the infant mortality rate was identical to the US numbers, 9 per 1,000 births. Thirty years earlier, international experts estimated Cuban baby deaths to be approximately 125 per 1,000. By the early 1990s the Revolution's aggressive medical care policies resulted in the average Cuban's life expectancy rising to seventy-five years, one year less than the American average. Once among the principal reasons for death, tuberculosis and infectious disease were relegated to positions below cancer, heart ailments and other top ten fatality causes. By 2002 the medical supply shortages threatened to jeopardise those achievements, but Cuban authorities continue to claim that the healthcare system is holding firm, combating the threat as successfully as the system's granite-nerved instigator, Fidel Castro, had repulsed CIA plots.

'We brag about healthcare whenever we have the chance,' Dr Sánchez said as he crossed to the refrigerator. 'This isn't exaggerated boasting. It's justified. No other low income country in the Caribbean matches our accomplishments.

Some day somebody will build monuments to Cuban medicine – towering obelisks with golden stethoscopes and syringes. I'm joking, but you get the idea.'

The refrigerator shelves were loaded with fruit, vegetables, goat's cheese and the roasted body of a chicken that was so scrawny it may have been a mercy killing. Dr Sánchez selected chicken parts and cheese for his plate. 'I never ate this well in the city. The farmers are eternally grateful we're here. Before this clinic was opened, the closest doctor was too far away to go and see.' Leaving the plate on the table, he walked into the bedroom. He came out with an envelope in his hand. 'This is for my father. I was planning on sending it tomorrow. The post office is slow –'

'And you'd like me to mail it in Canada. I'd be glad to. I've done it for people in the past. I was wondering about your work. The girl I drove here told me you visit patients on horseback.'

'In the mountains. My nurse and I try to go there once a month. It isn't easy to slip away. We have one hundred and twenty families under our care, and those families have many children. It's a big hive and we're busy little bees.'

'Is there a single problem you encounter more in the remote areas than you do in this village?'

'Ignorance. It's everywhere – villages, towns, cities – but the deeper you go into the mountains, the more you bang up against.'

By ignorance, Dr Sánchez was referring to a lack of fundamental knowledge concerning matters like personal hygiene and the spreading of household germs. Patients were advised that parasitic ailments could be contracted by walking about barefoot outdoors, and that consuming meals without washing their hands was a risky practice. Goats, dogs and chickens went in and out of mountain huts whenever it suited them: at a peasant domicile, Dr Sánchez saw a pig sleeping under a sick infant's bed. Mountain streams were the sources of drinking and cooking water. Dr Sánchez emphasised the importance of boiling the water to rid it of dung bacteria.

Enlightenment was a two-way street. An elderly female patient suffered from a chronic back problem and the availability of pain-relieving drugs was sporadic. On one of his regular mountain trips, the patient imparted the news that she no longer required the medicine the doctor prescribed, because she had found another method to control the pain. She had gone to a Santería priest and was now using a herbal concoction. Dr Sánchez had deemed Santería to be superstitious rubbish and herbal remedies a peso-wasting sham. But the concoction was helping the woman, and steeped in sullen reluctance, he dropped by the *santero*'s house to question him about the herbs he blended for the elderly woman. The *santero* gave him the names of three villagers he swore had ailments alleviated, if not cured, by herbal medicine. The patients verified the *santero*'s contention and, his reluctance vanquished, Dr Sánchez started compensating for drug shortages by utilising the *santero*'s services. He discovered which herbs to gather in the mountains or to acquire from city sources and what dosages to administer. He planted a herb garden. Attending a healthcare conference in Havana, he confessed to a group of doctors over dinner that he was treating patients with herbal remedies. To his surprise, some of his colleagues disclosed that drug shortages had propelled them on to an identical course.

'I still think Santería's a load of rubbish,' Dr Sánchez said, 'but herbs help patients suffering from minor illnesses, and I'd be a poor excuse for a doctor if I turned my back on that.' He had cleaned off the lunch plate while we were conversing. Now he was at Anna Karenina, refilling the plate with more chicken and cheese. 'Are you sure you don't want a bite? Some fruit, maybe?'

'No, I really must go.'

'Thank you for mailing the letter. My father will be glad to know his boy is alive and kicking.'

The waiting room was empty. The semi-blonde nurse was nowhere to be seen; a woman with tumbling black hair sat at her desk. Going to the car, I was pleased to learn that no one had swiped a souvenir. I passed the nurse on the road to the highway. I braked, backed up and offered her a lift.

'Wonderful,' she said. 'I'm completely exhausted. I was awake the whole night with a sick child. You driving north? Good. I live in the first town up the highway.' She sank onto the seat as though she intended to devote the rest of her life to sitting there. 'If I fall asleep, don't forget to wake me. I can't stand Havana. I'm dead against winding up there.'

'Did you run out of patients? I walked into the waiting room and there wasn't a soul in sight.'

'We shut for a while in the afternoons. When you were seeing Dr Sánchez, I looked after five people. Three shots, one blood test and an unmarried woman eager to know if she's pregnant because her sister is and they drank water from the same bottle. It boggles the brain. Hours and hours of reproductive health lessons in the schools and some women still believe the silliest things.'

'Cuba has millions of Catholics. Convincing people to use birth control must be a losing battle.'

'It isn't. Religion ends at the bedroom door. Catholics are as against unwanted babies as anybody else. They're using the loop. Condoms are expensive. The government did hand them out free but it can't afford to do that anymore.' Abortions were free too, but the government was attempting to lower the number of women having them by distributing loops and birth control information through institutions like the Family Doctor Clinics.

'Machismo. That's the problem on this island. Machismo.'

'In what way?'

'Every way. Condoms were free and men refused to wear them. And women did whatever the men said. Men run Cuba. They strut like roosters and hang around together like a pack of homosexuals. To a Cuban man, women are mothers or whores, and the woman hasn't been born yet who is as smart as the dumbest man.'

The National Assembly had striven to alter the situation. Permanently lodged in the Constitution, the Family Code provision pledged equality between the sexes. Husbands were obligated to assist in housekeeping and child-raising duties, and failure to comply constituted grounds for divorce. That equality extended to the workplace where it was illegal to discriminate on the basis of gender, however, anti-discrimination laws were somewhat like pentimento paintings, with time, the original impression revealed itself despite the covering layer. Cuban women complained of token inclusion in upper-tier Party circles and a double-standard that turned a blind eye when men in government posts conducted extra-marital affairs whereas adulterous women were automatically fired.

'Machismo isn't a Cuban anomaly. It's well entrenched in Canada too. Our heroes are men who hit each other over the head with hockey sticks.'

'I don't know hockey. I know medicine. Women come to the clinic and the doctor says, "Take these pills." The women promise they will – if their husbands let them. There was this farmer's wife. She was in an accident. Her ankle was broken and Dr Sánchez worried something else was wrong. He stuck her in the overnight room. The husband arrived at the clinic with meat and vegetables. He received permission to use the doctor's stove. Ten minutes later, the man comes into the kitchen holding his wife up. Every step's hurting her. Cooking's a woman's job, the husband says, and it's up to his wife to fix his meal.' The nurse swung her face away from me, as if gazing at a man was an unpleasant experience. 'Machismo,' she said quietly. 'Machismo, machismo.'

chapter twenty-one

Stepping off the lift, Jimmy Jazz radiated respectability. He was attired in a dark blue suit and a grey and blue striped tie that implied expensive schooling and Old Boy connections. He gripped a chocolate-brown briefcase, monogrammed with the initials of his real name. He was short and compact, his face was clean shaven, his blond hair scissored to perfection. Visually, he fitted right in with the international businessmen hopping about the Hotel Nacional lobby like hungry birds, the banking, hostelry and mining promoters hunting prosperity in the under-exploited land. In truth, Jimmy Jazz's trade was substantially different from theirs: he was a professional smuggler.

'You're going to be bored stiff,' he cautioned as we proceeded to a taxi parked at the side of the hotel driveway. 'He'll go blah, blah, blah and I'll go blah, blah, blah and that will be it. Doing deals is talking numbers. No thrills, my friend. Nothing to race the blood.'

'Not like crossing borders.'

'You'd better believe it. Every nerve in your body's tighter than a mosquito's ass. A customs guy stares you in the eye, you stand your ground and stare back. Your eyes swear you're a solid citizen, a church-going father of two. The kind of guy who uttered a dirty word when he was a kid and he's been begging God's forgiveness ever since. There was this family of tightrope artists, the Wallendas. Polish or German.'

'I saw them on television. German.'

'A reporter asked the family patriarch, a man in his seventies, why he wasn't retiring. "The wire is life," Karl Wallenda said. "Everything else is waiting." My life's crossing borders.'

Jimmy wouldn't discuss his childhood in detail. He said he was born in Winnipeg and his ultra-conservative father amassed a fortune running an unspecified commercial enterprise. Jimmy was a black sheep. He bailed out of the University of British Columbia to smoke dope and play the saxophone in a Vancouver band, the source of his Jimmy Jazz street name. He drifted to Mexico, and margaritas stunning his brain, he'd smuggled a kilo of marijuana into Texas. Waking up in a seedy El Paso hotel, he was appalled by his own foolishness. He had gone through the border with scraggly hair, tattered jeans and a drunken glow on his face. Everybody knew the border guards were predominantly clean-cut ex-Marines. He was lucky he hadn't been searched and busted. That day in El Paso, he vowed he'd never cross a border again unless his head was clear and he resembled a pure-living, law-abiding middle-class type.

Jimmy didn't smuggle dope anymore. In the 1990s he switched to South American gems, Asian artefacts and the fast-expanding trade that drew him to the Caribbean: Cuban cigars. North American cigar sales had experienced a 40 per cent increase in recent years: the Cigar Association of America estimated smokers spent roughly $60 million on good quality stogies. Toronto tobacconist Thomas Hinds reported that he could sell 20 per cent more Cuban cigars than he received. A thirty-year veteran of the tobacco business, Hinds said the Cuban industry, burdened by crop-damaging storms and restricted access to basic farming materials, fell millions of cigars short of meeting the global demand. Consequently, retail prices soared, enticing an increasing number of criminals who passed cheap stogies off as expensive items. In the tobacco trade they're called counterfeiters.

'Some of them are real dull blades,' Hinds said. 'A guy walked into my shop with a box of cigars he claimed were Davidoff Perignons. The stamp on the box bore a date that came four years after Davidoff ceased manufacturing that particular brand.'

How did cigars, long the ugly duckling of the tobacco industry, burst out of the back rooms to seduce the masses? Credit Hollywood. Credit Arnold Schwarzenegger, Bruce Willis, Robert De Niro, Clint Eastwood and other luminaries whose smoking habits trumpeted the New Truth that despite their unappealing aroma, despite the cancer peril, stogies were glamorous, stogies were cool. And not only for men. Sharon Stone, Whoopi Goldberg and Lauren Hutton lit up in step with a troop of fashion models, pop singers and LA bimbos. Enthused Hutton: 'Smoking cigars makes you feel worldly.'

Catching sight of the blossoming trend, Marvin Shanken launched a glossy magazine, *Cigar Aficionado*, in 1992. The New York-based quarterly succeeded to such an extent that early issues, selling out on news-stands, are now collectors' items. Editor and publisher Shanken has been a sharp-toothed critic of the Clinton administration's continuance of the Cuban trade embargo. In the spring of 1996, he published an article by Wayne Smith in which the former

State Department authority on Cuban affairs declared, 'If we can lift the embargo against Vietnam, extend most-favoured-nation treatment to China, and negotiate with North Korea, why can we not show some flexibility towards Cuba?' *Cigar Aficionado*'s opposition to the embargo has a self-serving aspect. Shanken contends that Cuban cigars are the smoothest on earth and it rankles him to know that they can't be purchased legally anywhere in the United States.

By stimulating North American smokers' appetite for the Cuban product, Shanken indirectly helped spawn a business opportunity for the likes of Jimmy Jazz. Havana stogies generally fetch up to $900 for a box of fifty in under-the-counter transactions. Jimmy smuggled authentic Cuban cigars into Canada and the United States, but the fattest profit came from his speciality: counterfeits.

In the taxi crossing Havana, Jimmy unbuttoned his suit jacket and loosened his tie. He couldn't stand the humidity, he said. West Coast drizzle was more to his liking. On La Rampa, he noticed a tourist peering into a plastic bag held by a middle-aged Cuban.

'Cigars,' Jimmy said. 'That buzzard works this street night and day. Two bucks a cigar. Fifty bucks a box of twenty-five. Haggle long enough and he'll drop the price to forty bucks. He swears they're real Cohibas – his wife works at the factory and gets them cheap. They're real, all right. Real fakes. Clowns like him are everywhere in this city. Caveat emptor. If they're selling you something that goes for three hundred bucks at the factory retail store, there's no way you're going to score it for forty.'

The taxi delivered us to a beaten old block of flats. Jimmy motioned towards circular gouges in the façade and said,

'Bullets. That's how proud Cubans are of their Revolution. Nobody fills in the holes. In Canada we've got public plaques, in Cuba they've got bullet holes.'

Jimmy wouldn't set foot in the lift. 'Tourist hotels have emergency generators. The power goes off in this dump, and we'd be in the elevator till Havana freezes over.' Climbing the stairs, he shed his jacket. At the fourth floor, he wiped his sweaty face with a silk handkerchief, tightened his tie and put the jacket on.

Tito and his wife, Valerie, were jittery. Jimmy had been sent by a third party, and in a milieu where informers inform on informers, they were apparently concerned that the impeccably attired stranger could be an undercover agent. Jimmy's unfriendly attitude was certain to inflame their nerves. Open and warm with me, he turned cold the moment he stepped into the flat. He ignored Tito's outstretched hand and he brushed off Valerie's invitation to have coffee.

'What are you peddling?' he asked bluntly. 'Where's the stuff?'

Tito took us into the kitchen. A handful of cigars were laid cheek by jowl on a Formica table. Jimmy sniffed and examined them. He didn't ignite any; he was a non-smoker.

'Not bad,' he said. 'We can do business.'

'What's your price?' Valerie asked from the doorway.

Jimmy acted as though she hadn't spoken. 'I'll quote you a price after you tell me how many cigars you can supply,' he said to her husband.

'How many would you want?'

'Four to five thousand.'

Tito was taken aback. He patted his thinning hair with his hand. His fingernails were stained brown, a condition common to cigar factory rollers who smoked while they worked. 'Four to five thousand,' he said uncertainly.

'It isn't worth chartering a boat out of Florida without a large shipment. Can you handle it?'

'Sure. No problem.'

The two men agreed on a price and a rendezvous date.

Descending the stairs, Jimmy was agitated. 'A waste of time,' he said. 'It was written all over his face. Tito won't come up with four thousand. It's bloody hard developing sources here. Cubans are too damned patriotic. They think of breaking the law, they think they'd be hurting the country too much if they did it on a big scale. I know Tito's type. He'd be content selling three boxes. It costs more for me to operate in the Dominican Republic, but those buzzards can fill merchandise orders.'

'Is there a good market for Dominican cigars in the States?'

'Not good enough. I smack Cuban bands on them. Cohibas are in hot demand. The average smoker doesn't appreciate the difference. You tell him a second-rate Dominican's a first-rate Cuban, and he'll smoke it and tell his pals Cuban cigars are extraordinary. Some smokers realise they're fakes and they don't care. To them, the big thing is showing off the Cuban band and basking in their friend's envy. How bored were you?'

'I wasn't. It went quickly.'

The taxi was waiting. Jimmy held the door open for me. 'I've been reading up on the history of Cuban cigars,' he said. 'It goes back to Christopher Columbus. He was the first person to smoke them.'

Whatever it was he had been reading, he was misinformed. Cigars were being smoked on the island ages before Columbus raised anchor. In November 1492, the great explorer wrote in his diary that members of a landing party encountered Indians indulging in a weird activity ... '[the Indians] carried firebrands and herbs dried and wrapped in a leaf that is dried and rolled like a musket, then lighted at one end while they suck or absorb or inhale the smoke from the other end.'

Columbus may or may not have tried *cohiba* (tobacco in the local Indian dialect), but a fifteenth-century French diplomat, Jean Nicot, did. He encouraged the Queen of France, Catherine de' Medici, to smoke and her zealous usage of the plant caused it to be dubbed 'the Queen's herb'. Sir Francis Drake introduced tobacco to England, and in the eighteenth century a Swedish botanist named the plant *Nicotiana Alata*.

Under Spanish rule, the Cuban tobacco trade prospered. The plants were cultivated throughout the country, but Spanish landowners discovered that the highest quality leaves grew in the red clay ground of Pinar del Río province. The harvested crops were dried in open-sided, thatched-roof sheds facing east to snare the morning sunlight. That tradition hasn't changed. The sheds are still utilised, but many farmers dry the *capas*, the outer leaves the tobacco is wrapped in, under vast cheesecloth sheets to protect them from wind and direct light. At the Havana factories, the leaves are inspected for defects and arranged according to colour and dimension by female workers, who, seated at tables, pile them on their laps. A crude Cuban joke has it that the tastiest cigars are those that were located closest to the workers' vaginas. Nobody jokes about the rollers. Among the most revered professionals in Cuba, master workers cut and hand roll between eighty and one hundred and twenty cigars a day. To lessen the monotony of their task, a fellow worker sits on a factory-floor platform and reads *Granma*, political tracts and pulp novels aloud.

Cruising away from Tito and Valerie's flat, I tried exposing Jimmy to some of that information. He cut me short. He obviously felt whatever reading he had done constituted all he needed to know about Cuba.

'John F. Kennedy smoked H. Upmanns,' he said. 'Before he lowered the embargo boom, he stored a thousand in the White House basement. I venture to say that if he wasn't shot, he would have depleted his provision and lifted the embargo to lay his hands on more H. Upmanns.'

The Nacional was nestled on a Malecón promontory. A tribute to colonial elegance, the 72-year-old hotel was, in its glory days, the temporary residence of choice for Winston Churchill, Ava Gardner, Marlon Brando and innumerable Mafia titans. Castroites had converted it into a block of flats: a tenant was evicted for disregarding the manager's multiple requests to get rid of his pet rooster. Now rooster-free and exquisitely restored, the Nacional was once again the favourite hangout for the wealthy and people on expense accounts behaving as if they were wealthy.

Jimmy, a six-figure income earner, invited me up to his room. He had a 'precious treasure' in the briefcase he lugged everywhere because he didn't trust the hotel staff. 'You ought to see this,' he said. 'It will aid in your research.' He opened the briefcase. It was stuffed with cigars. 'Partagá Robustos,' he beamed. 'None finer, my friend. A government big shot has a lung problem and can't smoke. I acquired them for a fabulous price. Limited edition. Extremely rare. In New York they'll bring fourteen thousand dollars.'

'How will you smuggle them past customs?'

'Simple. I'm the contented owner of a phoney receipt. On paper, they're worth one hundred dollars. The gentleman these are destined for has a sophisticated mouth. I couldn't fool him with a counterfeit.'

Refined taste buds weren't the sole requirement for spotting a bogus Cuban cigar. In many cases the lithographing on the bands was of poor quality, the boxes weren't constructed wholly of cedar (some had plywood bottoms) or the labels and stamps were attached in the wrong spots. Countless low-grade cigars had holes in the ends or plastic tips, and the leaves were clumsily rolled.

'This clown sidled up to me in a Manhattan bar,' Jimmy said. 'I laughed in his face. He was trying to sell a box of authentic Romeo y Julietas – rolled by a machine.'

Jimmy had never been apprehended smuggling cigars, counterfeit or the genuine article. He was confident Canadian Customs would merely fine him and confiscate the few boxes he occasionally transported on charter flights. American Customs was another matter. Hauling a large shipment of counterfeits by boat to Florida from Cuba or the Dominican Republic could reap a twelve-year prison term and a $250,000 fine. Jimmy had been jailed once in his lengthy career. He had been caught smuggling a Cambodian artefact, but dispensing bribes like sweets, he was permitted to flee his cell before his case went to court.

'Gems are a smuggler's dream,' he said. 'You swallow them, you shit them. You don't like the client who's paying your fee, you forget to wash them before delivery.'

A Cuban man came to the door. Jimmy didn't ask him in. Their conversation was *sotto voce*. The man waved his hands and sounded defensive. After he went away, Jimmy unscrewed a Havana Club bottle and rounded up drinking glasses.

'A second deal down the drain,' he said. 'The guy at the door said gasoline and fertiliser rationing is hurting tobacco farmers. Crop sizes are diminishing. Thirty million fewer cigars today than ten years ago.' He fixed me a drink and then folded his compact frame onto a chair. 'Ah, to hell with it. I'm flying home Sunday and I won't be coming back. It's too damn hard making a dishonest living in this country.'

chapter twenty-two

From Jimmy Jazz's bright, air-conditioned room at the Nacional, I went to Carlota's humid and cheerless flat for dinner. She was cooking rice and black beans, a Cuban food staple she referred to by its country-wide nickname, Moors and Christians. She mixed tiny slices of leftover meat in with the rice; pork, I hoped, and not something that purred. While she was setting the table, Roberto entered the kitchen and said to his mother, 'García's got a telephone.'

'How'd that happen?'

'Feathered friends flock together. The Party faithful rewarding the Party faithful. Nobody else in his building's got a phone.'

'Who'd want a phone?' Carlota scoffed. 'The police listen in and scribble notes. You'd close your mouth after you said hello and you wouldn't open it until it was time to say goodbye.'

'I can't see them doing that,' Roberto said. 'How many phones are there in Cuba? Hundreds of thousands. You can't tell me the police listen to all of them.'

'Maybe they don't listen, but everybody thinks they do, which is why Cubans lead the world in banal telephone conversations. Caution reigns supreme.'

Roberto plopped down on a chair. 'Miami radio was good last night. There were Canadian singers. Celine Dion. Polanka. Bryan Adams.'

'What's Polanka?' I asked. 'Polish music?'

'Canadian. "You're Having My Baby". Polanka.'

'Paul Anka.'

'Right. That's the guy.'

Carlota shook her head. 'You and your radio. I'll be glad when you get a new girlfriend and don't stay up half the night.'

'The girlfriend I get will listen with me. If she doesn't, she's out the door.'

Carlota bent down to retrieve a dropped fork. As she straightened, her eyes went strange and she grabbed the edge of the table. Roberto sprang upright.

'I'm OK,' she said. 'I'm a little dizzy, that's all.'

'Are you sure?'

'Yes, yes. Sit down. I'm not going to fall over dead.'

'Mother, go to the doctor. This isn't your first dizzy spell.'

'He'll send me to the hospital for tests,' she said. 'I won't go there. Never again.'

'She was in the hospital,' Roberto said. 'She was really sick and the room she was in –'

'Roberto, he doesn't want to hear it.'

'Actually, I was wondering what's going on in the hospitals.'

'Filth,' Carlota said, preparing to transfer the Moors and Christians to plates. 'What's going on is filth. Let me finish serving this, then I'll fill your ear with stories.'

Under Batista and his predecessors, the poor lacked the money to pay for healthcare. Most peasant farmers only worked for four months, and stretching pesos to last through the year meant denying themselves and their families doctors' visits and medicine. Growing up on his father's lucrative farm, Castro witnessed children with rickets and other serious ailments going untreated.

'Public hospitals, which are always full, exclusively accept patients recommended by powerful politicians,' he said in a 1953 statement, 'who, in turn demand the electoral votes of the unfortunate one and his family. Thus, Cuba continues forever in the same deplorable condition.' Within a year of deposing Batista, Castro ordered a wide-ranging overhaul of the medical system. Approximately 50 per cent of the nation's doctors fled the country: those remaining behind agreed to go on the government payroll and to provide their services free to the general populace. When food rationing was introduced in 1962, children suffering from malnutrition and other people with special needs were accorded extra portions. Castro was a miracle-worker. The instances of deaths from tuberculosis, parasites and most poverty-linked ailments shrank to record low levels.

In the mid-1990s, reports began leaking out of Cuba that, while the healthcare wasn't rapidly plummeting towards its pre-Castro status, the bloom was definitely off the rose. In 1993 a mysterious epidemic had afflicted nearly 51,000 Cubans. The symptoms included a high fever, a prickly feeling and bodily pain, weight and vision loss, and in many instances, the inability to walk without being physically supported. The World Health Organisation studied the outbreak, and failing to pinpoint a specific cause, concluded that nutritional deficiency was probably a major factor. Whatever the source was, the three-year-long epidemic dried up as mysteriously as it had started: since 1993 only the occasional case has been reported. Nevertheless, with food shortages steadily worsening, international health experts forecast an increase in nutrition-related ailments in Cuba and a gradual decline in overall medical standards.

The spread of the mystery disease was a sensational

incident that caught the foreign media's eye, largely due to the initial dread that a devastating new virus was responsible. As far as I knew, no media light had ever been shone on an enormously less dramatic event, the situation facing the average person entering hospital in Cuba.

An average person like Carlota.

At the dinner table, Carlota disclosed her apprehension over the calibre of medical care she'd receive when her physician treated her malady, 'a female disease'. At his office, he was, in her words, 'a train wreck of a human'. His eyes were bloodshot, his shoulders stooped, he mumbled and he called her Señora Sánchez, another patient's name.

'I said to myself, "Ah, he's having a lousy day." I went to Cuatro Caminos a couple of weeks later and there he was. His family were selling vegetables, and he was working at the stall. He had other part-time jobs too, assisting people at night. He couldn't survive on his state salary, fourteen dollars a month. A friend of his, a brain surgeon earning sixteen dollars a month, was working as a waiter because he earned more than that in tips every week. My doctor had part-time jobs and was fatigued. What were the nurses and doctors at the hospital doing? Were they moonlighting? Patients deserve total devotion to treating their illness. Alicia Alonso dedication.

'Did I receive it? Who knows? Some of the hospital staff had part-time jobs, but I don't know who did and who didn't. The point is, I went into the place filled with anxiety over the kind of care I'd be getting and anxiety is the enemy of good health. The day I arrived, I knew I had a valid reason to be worried. No, not about the part-time jobs, about the hospital itself. Filth everywhere. The floors were filthy, and the walls, and the stairways. Laundry soap was in poor supply and the bed things were stained and not washed right. Roberto took my pillowcases and sheets home on Saturdays to wash them. There was no hand soap and the towels were rags. Roberto brought me soap and clean towels, and I'd go into the bathroom and wash myself. There were three women in the room with me. Roberto wrapped the soap and took it home because someone might be tempted to steal it.

'The plates and drinking glasses were no cleaner. Smudges on the glasses and tiny bits of dried food on the plates. My doctor told me before I went to the hospital to bring my own knives, forks and spoons. The hospital stopped handing out cutlery when the patients and staff stole it. The meals? Cubans will eat practically anything, but hospital food was crap your dog wouldn't swallow. Roberto cooked for me. He brought my meals on the bus and I was glad to eat them, hot or cold. All those precautions, and I was struck down by a bad germ. I was sweating and throwing up and I was too weak to walk. The doctors had hardly any drugs – some days there was no aspirin on the entire floor – and I was stuck in my bed for three weeks until I finally shook it off. The woman next to me was in pain. When she craved strong medicine and there was none, they wheeled her to a storage room in the basement. She could scream there without driving us crazy.

'The hospitals are a disgrace. And the district clinics – a second disgrace. A woman at my office was three months' pregnant and went to a clinic. No examination gloves, no pills, no disposable syringes. The X-ray and ultrasound machines were broken and covered in dust. She had her baby, and it weighed five pounds. Five pounds! That's happening all the time. Underfed mothers are giving birth to small babies. We're becoming a nation of pygmies! The next generation will be so minuscule they won't sail to Florida on rafts, they'll mail themselves in packages!

'Why am I joking? It isn't a laughing matter. The ugly fact is, not all Cuban hospitals are horror houses. Frank País is sparkling clean and the medical equipment is first-rate. Frank País doesn't exist for ordinary folk, creaky old dancers like me. Who goes there? Foreigners paying special fees and Cubans on the government's favourite citizens' list. For thirty years after Batista ran to Santo Domingo, we were all equal, but now I'm sorry to report, there are again two classes of people in Cuba.'

When Carlota finished her rant, Roberto said it was a crying shame Cubans couldn't fly to the United States for medical care. 'Baseball's behind it. Silly *yanqui* pride.'

I said the connection between hospitals and baseball eluded me.

'Baseball's the cornerstone of America. The embargo bars us from American hospitals. Kill the embargo and Cuban teams would be on American soil beating the *cojónes* off their teams. Cubans winning the World Series. The *yanquis* couldn't stand the humiliation and they won't kill the embargo.'

Whether Cuban teams could whip the ass off the Americans was arguable. I had been to a ball game in Pinar del Río, however, and I knew Cuban fans matched, and possibly surpassed, American spectators when it came to straight-from-the-heart exuberance.

chapter twenty-three

It rained on the day I was supposed to go to the baseball game. A downpour soaked the streets of Pinar del Río and darkened the interior of the house I was in. Thunder cracked, lightning spat, the clouds above the suburb were uniformly desolate. 'Too bad,' I said dejectedly. 'I was looking forward to the game.'

Rosa's widowed sister, Lina, and her wiry, affable son, Paco, resided in the house. Pinar del Río was a tobacco-belt centre near the western tip of the island, and at Rosa's urging, I was spending time at the unadorned single-storey dwelling where the sisters grew up. Lina had gone to her hospital job before the rain began, and Paco, taking a day off, was kneeling on the living room floor, replacing the unreliable brake on his Flying Pigeon bicycle. He was sick of slamming into cars and buildings and chipping his teeth.

'Are you familiar with the Book of Genesis?' he asked.

'I've read it.'

'It says in Genesis that God created the earth and mankind in six days and then rested,' Paco said, attaching the brake cord to the frame. 'False. A gigantic lie. On the seventh day, He created baseball. The rain will stop. The field will dry. God understands the game's too essential to the human race to stop it.'

I doubted that God and the vast majority of the human race considered the sport that essential. I had no doubt

Cubans did. It was a source of patriotic ego gratification (the Cuban team, to use Roberto's phrase, was beating the *cojónes* off their opponents at the Olympic Games) and playing in the national league wasn't far behind having sex with a Pamela Anderson lookalike as the average male's leading fantasy. Barrio youngsters clouted tennis balls with sawn-off mop handles and Castro faithfuls reminded you that in the 1940s, El Jefe was a University of Havana pitcher whose fastball captivated American scouts. Talking baseball was almost as popular as going to stadiums. Fans regularly assembled in small groups on urban street corners and in public squares to discuss the sport. Occasionally the congregations were infiltrated by undercover agents checking to see if the participants were engaging in political scheming: it was said, rightly or wrongly, that agents volunteered for the assignments – they were keen on talking baseball.

Some Cuban fans believed baseball was solidly entrenched in the national psyche because it had been around for hundreds of years. Before Columbus sailed, the Tanío Indians competed against each other by belting crudely made balls and running to a base. That, the fans said, awarded Cuba the right to claim it invented the game, an assertion positive to rankle many Americans.

Whoever invented the sport, Cubans' attachment to it was astounding. There were 160 ball parks on the island (the largest, Havana's Latinoamericano Stadium, had 65,000 seats) and the raging demand for the product obliged the national league teams to play 120 games a season.

Baseball was alchemy. Innumerable North American writers have eulogised the sport's magical effect on spectators, but you had to be at a Cuban game to fully appreciate how wondrously dross can be converted into gold. Battered by poverty and bored by the general drabness of society, fans crowding the stadiums basked in golden light deflecting off the likes of the Lunatic, the Boy, the Big Drum and Tony the Cat. Enhancing the game's appeal was the freedom it granted to release repressed feelings in orgiastic eruptions.

Fulfilling Paco's prediction, the rain ended and the playing field dried. I was among 26,000 people filing, free of charge, into Capitan San Luis Stadium to observe the drama of two arch-rivals, Pinar del Río and Havana, striving to belittle each other. The stadium was named after a steely rebel killed in Bolivia in 1967 fighting alongside Che Guevara. The captain's picture was on the outfield scoreboard, close by a billboard beseeching spectators to diligently defend the fatherland against imperialism. There were no commercial advertising signs, no hotdog hawkers, no Goodyear blimp hovering overhead. It was a nostalgic spin backward to the era of low-gloss baseball, a time before players and, who knows, maybe even bat boys, acquired agents and lawyers and multi-million-dollar contracts.

We arrived forty-five minutes early. Paco's second prediction of the day was that the stadium would be packed, relegating latecomers to undesirable locations. Again, he was dead on. Latecomers nestled on the light stanchions and filled the space atop the patriotic billboards. Five men climbed over the short wall separating the stands from the playing field and huddled near the first base mound. A security guard ordered them to leave. Four obeyed. The fifth man waved his arms, argued and plunked himself down on the ground; two guards sprang from a dugout to lug him, Gandhi-passive, off the field.

'Who are the superstars I should watch for?' I asked Paco.

'We don't call them superstars.'

'OK. The greatest players.'

'The Boy, Omar Linares. He's the best. A hitting machine. He catches like silk. He'll be at third base – for Pinar del Río.'

The chattering, cigar-smoking crowd fell silent for a recorded rendition of the national anthem. Paco removed his Montreal Expos cap – he was a deputy manager for a government office doing business with a Quebec company – and held it over his heart. Havana trotted onto the field. The Rabbit was Pinar del Río's starting batter. Canadian fans generally take a few innings to warm up to the game, but not Cubans, not the enthusiasts at Capitan San Luis Stadium. The opening hit and the Rabbit's greased dash to first was a detonator. Leaping to their feet, fans screamed, blew trumpets and whistles, cheered and chanted. Two rows ahead of me, a stocky man had a bicycle pump hooked up to a trombone: he pumped and shouted, and at rare, quiet intervals during the game, a Three Stooges cry – whoop, whoop, whoop – whipped up his throat.

In the second inning, Pinar del Río grabbed a one-run lead. Havana tied the score in the third. When Havana shortstop German Mesa winged a fly ball into the stands, the fan catching it did what most Cubans did with fly balls – he helped the government economise by throwing it back to the field. At the bottom of the fourth, a Havana player bunted. The crowd was incensed. He was a renowned slugger and the outfield was playing him deep.

'*Cobarde!*' ('Coward!') somebody yelled.

'*Maricon!*' ('Homosexual!') somebody else bellowed.

'Your mother's children were born spineless!' the white-haired woman behind me contributed.

The teams were still tied 1-1 going into the fifth. Linares moved up to the plate. He uncorked a powerhouse swing that missed the ball. The crowd hollered encouraging words. A handbell rang, the trombone sounded. Linares shifted his stance, focused on the pitcher and met the second curveball with another mighty swing. The bat connected and the ball flew over the outfield fence. The crowd exploded. Amidst the noise, the hugging, the ecstatic leaps in the air, a middle-aged woman danced on a staircase landing, twisting her broad hips with the fervour and fluidity of a young girl.

Was this sport or a mass catharsis session?

I was reminded of my trip to China and the mountain rising above the city of Jinan. Early on a sunny morning, I had climbed the steps and followed the trails to the Buddhist temple at the summit. Men and women hidden in the heavy underbrush were shouting curses and loud pleas alluding to problems imposed upon them by lovers, neighbours, employers and party cadres. In a stiff-necked, overpopulated environment, the mountain was a spacious, socially acceptable place to let off steam. It was clear to me that the Capitan San Luis Stadium, and very likely every other national league stadium, was Cuba's version of the Chinese mountain.

'Which player's the Lunatic?' I asked Paco.

'Victor Mesa,' he said slowly.

'Is he playing tonight?'

'No.'

'Why's he called the Lunatic?'

Another pause. Paco's face twitched. 'He talks to himself.'

'Who's the Big Drum?'

'Orestes Kindelan. He's with Santiago.'

Paco's hesitation was understandable. He was thoroughly immersed in the on-field excitement and I was a distraction. The truth was, I hadn't come for the game, I had come for the atmosphere. I got to my feet, excused myself and went inside the stadium. A toothless woman and her teenage granddaughter were hawking *duro frio*, a yogurt and fruit dessert they'd made at their home. Not far away, a tall unshaven man glanced warily up and down the corridor, and opening a brown suitcase, revealed the contents to fans exiting the men's toilet. What was he selling? Cuban smut? I walked over. He was an artist, and breaking a regulation governing public sales, he was marketing pencil drawings of Omar Linares in action.

I had a question for him. Why didn't ordinary Cubans resent the fact that while they were scraping the financial bottom, Linares and his baseball clanmates were living high on the hog?

'Players earn fourteen dollars a month,' he said amicably. 'Go on a road trip and you'll know they aren't living high on the hog.'

It was true that the players were paid wages similar to those of average Cubans. And it was true they travelled in uncomfortable old buses to uncomfortable old stadiums (the Havana ball park was erected in the 1940s) where they slept in bunk-bed dormitories notorious for being smelly and cramped. Chicken, rice and beans were standard road fare. But there were perks that elevated certain players – the long-ball hitters, the strike-out aces – above and beyond the common person. *Sports Illustrated* reported that the Cuban luminaries were rewarded with new cars, swank houses, and in Havana pitcher Lazaro Valle's case, a free $25,000 renovation job on his house that included installing a pool and a dancefloor. International competitions and Latin American exhibition contests accorded the players enviable access to foreign goods, and for major stars such as Valle, cash bonuses of $5,000 were not unknown.

'You read it in an American magazine,' he sneered, 'then it must be absolutely accurate.'

'You don't believe it.'

'No, I don't. But if it is the truth, I don't care. Baseball brings honour and glory to our country. You know how many world championships we've won? Over twenty. Plus the Olympic medals. Let them live in palaces and drive nice cars – they deserve it.' He held up a drawing of the Boy leaping to catch a ball. 'You don't like these pictures? No, I read it in your eyes. I do them for extra pesos. I'll show you my real art. Come on.'

He closed the suitcase and led me to an exit.

'Where are your paintings?'

'Drawings. I don't paint. They're in the parking lot. Come on.' The crowd noise soared. 'A home run, I bet. We'll be quick. You won't miss much of the game.'

'It must be awfully tempting for Cuban players to defect. Rene Arocha rakes in millions of dollars playing in the States.'

'Who's Rene Arocha?'

'The pitcher. A ninety-four-mile-an-hour fastball. Ninety-four or ninety-six. Pretty damn fast, whatever it is.'

'The name means nothing to me.'

'You're kidding. He was a great hero in Cuba.'

'Defectors are traitors. We wipe their names from our memories. My car's over here.'

The well-preserved green and white Pontiac sat off by itself, as if it feared catching a rust virus from its fellow vehicles. I heard my wife's voice in my mind. 'Do you ever notice how people do unsafe things when they travel? They ride in overloaded boats with no life jackets and they take shortcuts down dark alleys. They remember to bring their jewellery and their cameras, but they leave their brains at home.' Going to an isolated part of a near-deserted car park with a total stranger was, it dawned on me, an excellent example of a traveller leaving his brain at home. The crime rate in Cuba was comparatively low, but people did get mugged, did get murdered.

A husky six-footer and a sharp-featured woman wearing a purple headscarf slid out of the Pontiac. The artist introduced them. The woman was his fiancée, the six-footer her brother. The lock on the trunk was broken and they were stationed in the car to guard the drawings, the spare tyre and the jack.

The drawings came in two variations of hideous. There were the ultra-ludicrous pictures of huge-bellied tourists with dollar signs floating above them, and slightly less hurtful to the eye, pictures of tiny, ebony creatures resembling Casper the Ghost.

The artist sought my opinion on which series was the best. I picked the Caspers.

'The *jigües*,' he said.

Jigües were legendary underwater people. When you were wading in the ocean and something dark suddenly scurried past, it was a 'little black person'. *Jigües* never harmed land-bound humans; they dined on minnows and seaweed.

I bought a *jigüe* for $5. A steep price for a piece of visual rubbish, but relieved they weren't muggers planning to challenge my skull with a tyre iron, I was happy to pay it.

Paco nodded and muttered a greeting as I reclaimed my seat in the stands. Then he sprang up and added his voice to the clamour of cheerful noise. A Havana baseman had dropped the ball. At the end of the game, feverish Pinar del Río fans celebrated the team's two-run victory by swarming on to the playing field, singing, dancing and blowing whistles.

Paco and I merged with the mob leaving the stadium. He didn't seem to notice that I had intentionally abandoned the rolled up drawing on my seat. We walked to his house. His mother was in the front room, mending a blouse by hand.

'We won,' Paco said joyfully. 'Those Havana guys are sissies.'

'Paco and baseball,' Lina said to me. 'Some days I think that's all he lives for.'

'It is,' her son teased, 'baseball, and my mother.'

Like her sister, Lina was short and pretty and smart. She hadn't Rosa's humour, and a disposition towards sombreness tightened the edges of her mouth and dulled her eyes. Paco was her only son. Two daughters had married and a third was living common-law. Within minutes of first meeting her, she told me she was glad Paco was an unrepentant ladies' man and had no inclination to wed – she would be devastated if he moved out.

'Paco's grandfather's responsible,' Lina said. 'He took Paco to games when he was little. In the past, Havana was a farm team for Cincinnati. My father collected chewing-gum cards. Photographs of Cincinnati players. He went to the factory one morning in 1962, and my mother burned them. She thought he was idolising the enemy. To this day, my father hasn't forgiven her.'

'Grandmother was mistaken,' Paco said. 'By collecting those cards he was lending his support to the Communist party. You remember the name of the American team, mother? The Cincinnati Reds. Obviously, a Marxist organisation.'

The joke was lost on Lina. She cut the thread and dropped the needle into the sewing basket. 'Miguel was a baseball star,' she said. 'Not professionally, for the university. That was how he met Rosa. He was waiting to bat and he looked in the stands. The moment he saw Rosa, he vowed he was going to marry her. After the game, still in his uniform, he ran into the stadium and accosted her.'

'So that's how they got together,' I said. 'He didn't tell me.'

Lina rose and walked to her bedroom to hang the blouse in the wardrobe. 'The new planter's here,' she said to her son.

Paco and I went into the backyard. He switched on the patio light, a naked hanging bulb. The new planter was a toilet bowl filled with dirt and flowers. It matched the ornamental container already there, a cracked flower-crammed bathtub. Nothing in Cuba was wasted; the country must have had the world's smallest rubbish dumps.

'Where did my grandfather pinch this?' Paco said. 'His neighbour's bathroom?'

He glanced inside the house to make sure his mother wasn't listening. 'My uncle's a great guy – I'm not criticising him – I'm setting the record straight. He was a good fielder, but he couldn't hit worth dog shit. He lasted one season.

And he didn't run into the stadium to woo my aunt. He was near the dugout and the guy at the plate threw his bat. It struck Miguel and he fell down. Rosa was in the front row. She was a first-aid volunteer and she jumped onto the field. My uncle was woozy from being hit by a bat, not from the sight of Rosa in the stands. Rosa's told my mother she has the story wrong, but my mother won't change it. Sibling rivalry. Rosa was forever correcting her in childhood, so she'll tell the story wrong, knowing it's wrong, rather than admit her sister was right.'

chapter twenty-four

On our maiden trip to Cuba in 1986, my wife and I stayed in a bungalow on Irenee du Ponte's former estate, fifteen miles east of Havana. At least, I think we stayed on Irenee du Pont's former estate. A Cubanacán guide and a dining room waiter both said the two dozen houses had been confiscated from the Delaware chemical mogul. The desk clerk thought otherwise; he said the property had been owned by a New York gangster.

'Irenee du Ponte owned a gorgeous house in Varadero,' he said. 'It's still there, surrounded by hotels built on his private golf course. If these were his guest bungalows, he must have liked to keep his guests at arm's length. Varadero's an hour from here.'

Whatever their origin, the bungalows were airy, pastel, tile-floored gems. Erected in the 1950s, they spread across a shady hilltop, roughly half a mile up from the beach. Cubanacán ran an hourly shuttle bus to the seafront, but the buses were usually empty: hotel guests lolled around the swimming pool between escorted tours to Havana craft stores and museums.

One morning my wife and I were descending the steep hill to the beach, feeling privileged. Vancouver was drowning in rain, Toronto was snow-bound, the East Coast was slapped by sleet and shrieking winds. Below us, at Playas del Este, the ocean looked huge, smooth and sensuously blue. The road we were traversing was flanked by bushy fields. We passed a relaxed, revolver-wearing guard riding herd on a bunch of prisoners cutting brush with machetes. We had nothing to be alarmed about. The prisoners were convicted drunks and petty robbers; the Cuban justice system didn't support the concept of sticking machetes in the hands of murderers.

'Do you think the Bulgarians will be there?' Jessie asked.

'I don't know. I bet their tent won't be. Too big a hassle.'

The day before, we had been mesmerised by a group of Bulgarian men attempting to raise a canvas tent. The pegs loosened in the soft sand and the tent repeatedly caved in. They finally got it to remain upright, but none of them went inside. The weather was too nice. We gathered they planned to sleep in the tent that night, but at four o'clock they tore it down, stashed it in a minivan and drove towards Havana.

'I don't know a great deal about Bulgaria,' Jessie said. 'The capital's Sofia. Bulgaria exports cheap wine.'

'Wrestling's their national sport. Bulgarians are good at winning Olympic medals.'

'You're thinking of Turkey. Turkish wrestlers are good at winning medals. Don't pay attention to him and he'll go away.'

'Who?'

'The dog.'

I turned my head. A small, emaciated mongrel was close behind. I tried to heed my wife's advice, but the urge to glance over my shoulder was too strong. We walked a quarter of a mile, and the dog didn't go away. It dropped back, it ran into a field to chase a bird, but it didn't go away. Then it drew alongside me, trotting contentedly as though it were on an outing with its fawning master. It was a repellent beast. A distorted jaw and mangled ears, a near-hairless body pocked with sores. I was wearing shorts and when it brushed against my leg, I groaned, 'Oh, no, rabies for sure.'

'You can't get rabies unless he bites you. Ignore him. Dogs hate eye contact. Don't look him in the eye, and he won't bite.'

The dog accompanied us off the hotel road and across the highway onto the sand. We chose a place to spread our beach towels and sit; the dog plopped down a few yards behind us. There weren't many people on the beach. Five or six foreigners, perhaps ten Cubans. I stripped to my bathing trunks and went to the water to wash the dog's germs off my leg. The beast followed me.

I whirled and yelled, 'Get out of here! Menace somebody else!'

The dog wagged its tail.

A tall solidly constructed man in a faded plaid shirt rose from the sand and walked over to me. 'I take it this isn't your dog,' he said in English.

'It trailed us to the beach,' I said. 'We can't get rid of it.'

'The little bugger,' he said. 'A genuine pain in the rump.'

He crouched down and did something that was either brave or moronic, or both; he patted the dog's mangy head. Drawing himself erect, he slipped a bag of peanuts from his pocket, poured some onto his palm and encouraged the dog to gulp them. When the nuts were gone, the dog licked his hand.

'Let's go, buddy.'

The dog eagerly followed him up the beach, past a line of hurricane-damaged palm trees and into a hotel car park. Losing sight of them, I waded into the water.

Jessie joined me.

'Who was that guy?' she asked.

'He sounded American. A Midwestern drawl.'

'Where was he taking the dog?'

'Beats me. I hope it wasn't to our bungalow. I'll be in a three-vodka mood if it's sitting on the doorstep, wagging its tail.'

The Bulgarians didn't turn up. Nevertheless, I did have a beach show to observe. Three Italian women, svelte, blonde and haughty, stuffed their bikini tops in Gucci bags and walked back and forth to the sea, in spite of tourist guidebook warnings that topless bathing was considered the realm of promiscuous women, and Cuban men were liable to hiss and yell obscene remarks. The Cuban men passing the Italians leered and grinned, and a youth sat on the sand near them, unabashedly staring as if breasts were gold and he'd found the motherlode.

On our daily trips, we ate lunch at oceanside hotels rather than scale the hill for a prepaid meal. One afternoon we went into a bar and ordered Bucaneros. A man drinking by himself at the next table swung around to greet us.

'Aren't you the folks the dog was bothering?'

'That's right,' I answered. 'Thanks for taking care of it.'

'No problema.' He extended a hand. 'I'm Harry Anderson.'

Harry had a flat in Havana and he rode the wawa, the dilapidated intercity diesel bus, to Playas del Este once a week. Cubans were generally habitual drinkers (in those days, they could afford beer with breakfast and lunch, and rum with dinner) and Harry, a heavier drinker than most men, came to the beach because he liked the bars there. He told us that upon introducing himself. He also told us he was on holiday from his job translating government documents and writing news releases in English.

'I'm a piss-poor writer,' he said. 'I can string words into sentences, but the sentences I string are godawful. I have, in fact, the dubious distinction of writing one of the rottenest lines ever printed in *Granma*'s English edition. "The Minister of Agriculture, spiffy in an expensive, recently dry-cleaned suit and professionally shined shoes, announced that this year's sugar cane production rate was bigger than last year's." I was three sheets to the wind and I latched on to the suit and shoes bit gazing at the minister's photograph. *Granma* canned an editor for letting the story go to the printer's and my department hired an Englishman, a retired reporter, to check everybody's future releases.'

Harry was a Kansas farmer's son. Balding and square-faced, he slouched and complained and criticised: life, his words and manner insinuated, had booted and bruised him more than it did most people. His wry humour and generous nature (he helped Cubans with their English in letters they penned to foreigners) were his saving graces. Harry was part of a near-extinct species, a native-born American who had landed in Cuba during the Batista regime and never returned home.

'Havana was Little America in the fifties,' he said, ordering his third beer in the Playas del Este bar. 'Woolworth's department stores, Sloppy Joe's saloon. Coca-Cola and Wheaties. Cubans had their own Lions, their own Rotary Clubs. How'd I wind up here? I was handy with dice and I winged it from New York to work at the Riviera. Meyer Lansky's joint. The fanciest hotel in the Caribbean and he built it. To beat the taxman, he was listed on the payroll as a low-pay employee – kitchen staff superintendent. A riot, that was. Meyer Lansky, Mafia millionaire, kitchen staff superintendent.'

Harry married a Cuban woman, and guessing which way the political wind was blowing, he quit the Riviera months before Castro swept into the city. When El Jefe commenced an anti-American campaign in 1960 by nationalising US-owned companies, Harry felt certain he'd be deported. He didn't want to go; he loved his wife, a strident Castroite who, in his words, 'barfed at the notion of living in the States.' Fortunately, the Communists required translators, and he was hired by a government ministry. His marriage ultimately ended in divorce, and in 1983, at the age of 56, he wed a 23-year-old dental technician.

'I'm no knee-bending Christian, but in the old days I begged God to give me a purpose. I was drifting day to day, year to year. These days, I've got my purpose, keeping Marielena happy. I pull down good money and she doesn't want for much.'

'What did you do with the dog?' Jessie asked.

'I dumped peanuts on the back seat of a car and stuck him inside. He was feasting merrily the last I saw.'

Jessie looked slightly incredulous. 'You picked the closest car and shut the dog in it?'

'It wasn't like that. The guy driving it runs this hotel. He gave me a tough time last week. I reckon the dog's sleeping on the floor and the guy doesn't see him, and then halfway to Havana, the dog leaps up and chomps his neck. That'll teach the bastard.'

We met Harry frequently that summer. His negative attitudes notwithstanding, he was likeable and informative and we enjoyed the feeling we were engaged in something unique, consorting with a romantic character, a man who had abandoned his own country in an era of revolutionary upheaval for the love of a woman (even if that love did perish in a divorce court). Back in Canada, we received the odd letter from him. When our friend in Holguín, Miguel, wrote to us, he consciously avoided saying anything that might smack of anti-government sentiment. His suspicions about post office employees opening mail and reporting political dissidents necessitated bland accounts of family events and local weather. Harry shot from the hip. He blasted the growing unreliability of public transport, the food dilemma, the declining GNP statistics.

As a joke, I sent him a copy of *Will America Surrender?*, a 400-page, right-wing rant in which Chicago author Slobodan Draskovich implored the United States to regain its global supremacy by striking meaner blows against world Communism. Lambasting Cuba, Draskovich lamented his nation's 'timid and yielding policy' towards the Castro government. Six weeks after I sent the book, Harry wrote to me: 'The crush-the-enemy hysteria Draskovich spews hides the fact that Communists in Cuba despise American foreign policy, but they sure as hell don't despise America itself. Cubans are nuts for American consumer goods and the American lifestyle. These days, they're keen for running shoes and baseball caps. I recall the fifties when fur coats were all the rage because American women wore them. In this sultry land, restaurants and clubs installed air conditioners to woo the business of Cuban women wearing them. Given half the chance, Cubans would be satellite Americans and you wouldn't be able to tell downtown Santiago from downtown Syracuse.'

On our second trip, Jessie and I travelled to a coastal resort outside Cienfuegos. Harry came to spend five days with us. He was sorry we couldn't meet Marielena; she was ill, her mother was looking after her in Havana. Harry drank, haunted the pool area, went to the hotel disco. When we saw him, which wasn't often, we had lively, enjoyable conversations. The day before he flew home, we were relaxing in the bar and a Montreal accountant stopped by our table. A Cuban teenager had approached him on the beach and tried to sell him a bagful of pot. The youngster said the plant, Cubano Supremo, was locally raised. Harry had never smoked marijuana and he insisted he never would, yet he asked the teenager's name and what village he inhabited. The accountant couldn't answer either question.

Later that night in our room, Jessie said to me, 'I'm beginning to wonder about Harry.'

'Wonder what?'

'The questions about the kid selling pot. Harry always has money to spend and he seems to have been to every resort, and in every bar, foreigners frequent.'

'Maybe translators are paid well.'

'It isn't just those things. Cubans work six days a week. Not Harry. He's off more than he works.'

'You think he's a counter-intelligence agent? An informer?'

'Why not? Secret police employees are on the staff at tourist resorts. Every time a maid or a waitress or a shop clerk rubs shoulders with a tourist, there's the chance a dissident may reveal their true colours. Why not have somebody who can pass for a tourist mingle with the staff? Somebody who talks to them in a friendly way – and helps write their letters to foreigners.'

'And you claim I'm paranoid about the police here. Harry isn't a spy. I'd feel it in my bones if he was. Male intuition.'

In 1991 Harry flew to Santiago to meet us, Marielena at his side. She was quiet, delicate and roughly five feet in height. It didn't take long for me to register that Marielena was cursed with a perpetually restless nature: she absently fingered her sunglasses, she lit cigarettes, took several drags, butted them and stashed the remains in her purse. She went for solitary walks, she glumly surveyed her immediate surroundings as if she had felt since childhood that wherever she was wasn't the place she was meant to be.

Harry was his usual self, drinking, dispensing bits and pieces of wry humour, chatting with strangers. On a wet afternoon Jessie, who normally won't shop unless she has something specific in mind, reluctantly consented to go to a tourist mini-mall with Marielena to see what the shops stocked. Marielena bought a bathing suit and perfume; Jessie returned empty-handed.

'Marielena said something intriguing,' Jessie apprised me. 'We were discussing Harry's boozing and she mysteriously said, "There are worse things than drinking. Be careful what you say around him." I'm telling you, darling, Harry's a spy.'

I wouldn't accept that. Not without stronger proof.

I continued to exchange letters with Harry, two or three a year, and then he stopped writing. A letter I sent in 1994 was returned by the new tenant of his old flat, along with a note stating that Harry had moved to an unknown address.

Harry roamed the outskirts of my mind all the time I was in Havana. I phoned the ministry he claimed employed him. The department chief said there was no one named Harry Anderson currently in his department; he wouldn't confirm or deny that Harry was formerly on the staff there. Carlota and Roberto listened to my story. 'Shoot the *pendejo*!' Roberto howled. 'He's an informer!' His mother was kinder. 'If he's working for the security police, the poor man was probably forced into it. Why don't you go to Playas del Este? Drunks are creatures of habit. I'm sure he's drinking at the same bars.'

If Harry was drinking in the same Playas del Este bars, nobody knew him. Outside the Tropicoco Beach Club, the cosmetic new name adorning the grey-bearded Hotel Marazul, I recognised a taxi driver who had frequently driven Harry to his old flat. 'Señor Harry? He lives on my street. I can take you to the building.'

Harry resided in a high-rise ghetto on the eastern edge of Havana. The buildings were blockish and sterile, designed by Russian architects to advance the values of proletarian simplicity. Harry's flat was on the fourth floor. I expected him to be surprised and gladdened by my sudden appearance. He was surprised, but it swiftly became apparent he was lodged too deep in his own private hell to be glad.

'I've been planning to write to you,' he said unconvincingly.

The room was an affirmation of the simplicity ideal. Harry may have earned good money translating documents, but he didn't spend it on furnishings. I sat on a hard couch facing a bare wall. A box filled with used car parts lay on a basket chair; the last I heard Harry didn't own a car and wouldn't know how to drive it if he did.

'I don't have any coffee,' Harry said. 'I can offer you rum. Bootleg, home-grown by a Señor Martínez from the magnificent, all-purpose sugar cane plant. It's got quite a kick.'

'No thanks, Harry. I don't feel like being kicked today.'

'I can't buy the real stuff anymore. I'm retired and living on a government pension. If you call it living. In Kansas, the farm stock eat better.'

We half-heartedly discussed Cuba's myriad woes and then I asked how Marielena was.

'How should I know?' Harry said. 'She's gone.'

'Gone? You two split up?'

'Sort of. Excuse me a minute.' He went into the kitchen to fetch himself a glass of bootleg rum. 'It's a sorry tale,' he said, coming back and dropping onto a cracked rocking chair. 'You'll cry me a river hearing Marielena's problem.'

Marielena's problem was the condition sexologists currently labelled compulsive sexual behaviour disorder. The outdated, more accessible name for it was nymphomania. Psychiatrists had treated her and she had been hospitalised twice for depression. Harry, aware that Marielena had had multiple lovers prior to meeting and marrying him, was unaware that the tally was in the hundreds.

'There was this nympho in high school. She slept with everybody and anybody, and the guys laughed behind her back. I don't laugh no more. Nymphomania's a recurring illness, like malaria. It seizes you and you can't shake it off. Marielena does this vanishing act. She says she's going to the market or visiting a friend and then she doesn't come home. She can't hold on to a job because she meets some asshole and goes off with him. One time I woke up at three in the morning and she wasn't in bed. She'd snuck off somewhere.

'I'm at my wits' end. I can't concentrate on anything except her. You were lucky to catch me here. I'm always searching for Marielena. My illness is as bad as hers. I take our wedding picture and go about asking people if they've seen her. Lots of times she's in the neighbourhood, shacked up. Sometimes I find her and sometimes I don't. The times I do, she starts bawling the second she lays eyes on me. She swears she's sorry and it won't happen again, but we both know it's in her blood and regret can't destroy it. When I can't find her, I wander the streets, looking for her face. Marielena's unpredictable. She can screw a stranger and pick up and go two minutes later. It drives me loony when she shacks up for weeks and I can't find her and she doesn't come home till she's good and ready to. You know the worst part of it? Sex does nothing for her. Absolutely nothing. She's never had an orgasm. The psychiatrist hasn't been born yet who can figure that lady out.'

I sensed that Harry wasn't having a dialogue with me, he was having it with himself. He sketched striking pictures of soldiers and diplomats, labourers and students – of sex in deserted corridors, derelict houses, sparkling hotels and shabby bedrooms next to sleeping children. It didn't matter to Marielena whether the men were married or single, young or old, black or white. In recounting her carnal adventures, Harry was sadly, perversely, swimming in sweet agony.

As he rattled on, gulping rum and aiming the odd glance towards the couch, I listened to our friendship die. He said nothing of Marielena's infidelities in Santiago, nor did he even hint at them in subsequent letters. Why maintain a relationship with someone who, finally exposing his anguish, did so as though you were no one special to him, your presence no more than an excuse to feed an emotional addiction?

I never knew whether Harry was an informer or not, but I did know there was some truth to the proverb that the gods answer the prayers of those they wish to punish. Harry had prayed for a purpose in life, and perhaps gazing disapprovingly upon his earthly conduct, the gods delivered Marielena.

chapter twenty-five

'Chiclets! Chiclets!'

Recognising a foreigner when he saw one, the boy ran up to me with an outstretched hand. Begging had come to the tourist areas of Havana but this was a novelty, a freckled nine or ten-year-old working an apartment building corridor. On the streets, chewing-gum and dollars were the children's most common requests; adults, almost always female, pleaded for clothing. Why Chiclets, a chewing-gum of less than spectacular popularity in the rest of the world, were in vogue for Cuban kids was a puzzling state of affairs. It had to be a fifties' legacy, the blackjack and whore epoch when *yanquis* with overweight wallets felt like angels of mercy when they dished out chewing-gum to Havana urchins.

Roberto had no such feelings. He waved a stick of Juicy Fruit and said to the youngster grabbing at my arm, 'Little worm. Your mother did me a favour. Can you be kind to her today?'

'I'll be kind.'

'How kind?'

'I'll go to bed early tonight.'

'This is yours.'

The boy tore the wrapper apart. 'What number are you after?'

'Three hundred and two,' I answered.

'Señor González. He plays funny music.'

'I failed to notice the Juicy Fruit store in your neighbourhood,' I said to Roberto. 'There must be one, you have tons of the stuff.'

'Contraband. You want to hear a great story? Ask Tony about Santiago – a lady named Pilar.'

'Why? What's the story?'

'I can't tell it like he can. Trust me, he'll chill your blood.'

For a blood-chiller, Tony González was soft-spoken and personable, his flat painted bright yellow and blue instead of Vincent Price black. Edging into his sixties, he looked scholarly and dignified, a unique appearance for a jazz musician who gained most of his income playing pop tunes in boozy hotel lounges.

'This looks great,' Roberto said. 'Where'd you find the paint?'

'My brother,' Tony replied. 'He was on a government construction project. He has two tins of yellow – you interested in a trade?'

'Naturally. Does he drive? I can lay my hands on motor oil.'

Roberto had business with Tony. He was selling cassettes to the musician. A young man in Roberto's neighbourhood had obtained cassettes from an underground source, and making dozens of copies, sold them for a buck apiece. Roberto received a commission for the tapes he unloaded. Almost all of the music was American and British rock, but the occasional jazz cassette surfaced, and when it did, Roberto contacted Tony. Today, he was delivering several copies of a Bill Frisell tape the jazz musician had ordered for himself and his friends.

'Who is this guy? A trumpet player?'

'Guitar,' Tony said.

The title was hand-printed on the cassette cover. 'I have this,' I said. 'One of his best albums. He redid the score from a Buster Keaton film.'

Like Trekkies and Branch Davidian followers, jazz fans perceive themselves as members of a glorious, underappreciated movement. My remarks were a signal to Tony that we were fellow cultists, and as I had anticipated, he reacted favourably.

'A jazz fan,' he grinned. 'So it isn't true that the only music Canadians love are hockey songs.'

'Hockey songs? There aren't any. Unless Shania Twain records them – I have no idea what she does.'

'Who's Shania Twain?' Roberto asked.

Tony paid for the cassettes and Roberto left. Tony showed me his jazz collection. Heavy on vinyl Coltrane's and Dizzy's, light on more recent releases. 'There's an excellent programme on Havana radio but most of their material is ancient. Precious little beyond the 1960s. Don Byron, Matthew Shipp, Cassandra Wilson – we know their names but we don't know their music. We hear the blonde flautist sometimes. The Canadian. What's her name? Jane Bunnett. She's famous amongst Cuban musicians.'

Tony had written a book chronicling the history of Cuban music. The manuscript was gathering dust on a bureaucrat's shelf, awaiting a publication-approval command based upon its reverence for socialist principles and the availability of paper. He had submitted it five years ago.

'No, the delay doesn't upset me,' he said. 'Have you seen the lines outside the stores? For Cubans, waiting is a natural condition.'

It was Tony's book that had compelled me to have

Roberto set up an interview. Indigenous music rivalled baseball as an island-wide obsession. Within hours of learning to walk – or so it seemed – children swayed their hips to rumba rhythms. More than likely, Benny Moré lyrics formed sentences on their lips the day they uttered their first words. One night I was sauntering behind a female soldier on a Havana street. She was striding along, stiff-spined and square-shouldered. Passing a building where salsa music throbbed out of a window, she broke her stride, gyrated and vigorously twisted her hips. There were Cubans who couldn't dance, it was said, but their lack of rhythm was forgivable – they were dead.

'How extensive is your knowledge of Cuban music?' Tony inquired.

'I know the Afro-Cuban rhythms jazz musicians use go back to the slaves. And Pérez Prado was called the Mambo King because he invented the beat.'

'Pérez Prado was the Mambo King but he didn't invent the beat. Sit down. I'll get the coffee. I haven't the time to cover everything that's in my book, but I can tell you quite a bit. Tío Tom, for instance. I'm sure he's a stranger to you. He was *muy macho*. He stood up to the tyrant torturing Cuba before Batista.'

I was mistaken about Pérez Prado, but I got the slavery part right. Members of the Yoruba, the tribe that had introduced Santería to Cuba in the sixteenth century, enlivened their nights away from the sugar cane fields with drumming, singing and dancing. The songs were filled with references to Santería deities. Early in the nineteenth century, son, another African-derived musical form employing dance, percussion and singing, flowed out of former slave centres in eastern Cuba to garner popularity in Havana. Son looked and sounded primitive and profane to white Habaneros, and for many years it was officially banned. Since 1952, a semi-professional troupe based in an old pirate port near Havana, Los Muñequitos de Matanzas, has been travelling the world performing son music. Los Muñequitos draw respectable-sized audiences but their success outside of Cuba has been limited compared to the huge popularity enjoyed by another group of son musicians. In 1996 American guitarist Ry Cooder and a bunch of ageing local performers assembled in a Havana studio to record an album named after a defunct private club, the Buena Vista Social Club. Conga player and singer Compa Segundo was eighty-nine, pianist Ruben González seventy-seven. The album won a Grammy award and sparked the current vogue for Cuban music in North America.

Most foreigners are probably unaware of the fact that son is actually the original salsa, the womb in which the rumba was conceived, and that the rumba was the outcome of a mating between African and Spanish rhythms. There were three versions of the rumba: two originating in the countryside (*guaguanco* and *columbia*) and one with metropolitan roots (*yambu*). In all three the dance symbolised the eternal quest by men to win women's affections. An immensely admired poet, Nicolás Guillén, wrote protest verses assailing the status quo and its pitiless treatment of the poor. He included many references to the dance in his work and he was labelled 'the emperor of the rumba poets.'

Guillén put pen to paper in pursuit of literary excellence. Tío Tom's ambition was to scale a smaller peak – he sought to support his family writing pop songs. Calling himself Uncle Tom (his real name was Gonzalo Ascenio

Hernández), he turned out batches of appealing rumba tunes dealing with unrequited love, infidelity and other subjects that never go out of fashion. His social conscience was aroused in the 1940s when a group of drunken American marines desecrated the Martí monument in Havana. After a judge released the marines without punishment, Tío Tom produced a scorching rumba song accusing President Prío of kowtowing to a foreign government for the sake of money. He was convicted of sedition and served a six-month prison sentence.

Guillén's poetry and Tío Tom's music were Cuba-centric. They were not tailored to seek international attention. Jazz, on the other hand, automatically spoke with a global tongue: it was understood in Havana, New York, Sydney and Bombay. Cuban musicians picked up ideas listening to jazz geniuses like Louis Armstrong and Duke Ellington, and in exchange, they furnished American bands with a Latin influence. Trumpeter Chico O'Farrill did compositions for Benny Goodman and Stan Kenton, drummer Chano Pozo contributed Afro-Cuban arrangements to the Dizzy Gillespie Orchestra. Like hot spices, intrinsic Cuban musical expressions inspired by African tribal rhythms were sprinkled upon jazz pieces by both Latin and American composers.

In the late 1970s, an eight-piece Havana band, Irakere, pointed the music in a new direction. Led by pianist Chucho Valdéz, the band made the Afro-Cuban sound a prominent component of its work and not just an augmenting factor. The band lost its potency when two star musicians, trumpeter Arturo Sandoval and saxophonist Paquito D'Rivera, defected to the United States.

'Chucho's a great pianist,' Tony said. 'So are Gonzalo

Rubalcaba and Hilario Durán. For some reason, Cuba's blessed with exciting jazz pianists. I could go on all day. I haven't covered classical music or popular singers, but I'm sure you have enough material.'

'Pérez Prado. You said he didn't invent the mambo.'

'Benny Moré sang with the Pérez Prado band before he was on his own. He was a rare talent – mambo, son, rumba; he sang everything and anything as if he had a special gift for whatever he was doing at the time. I'm sliding off track. Pérez Prado – he claimed to have fathered the mambo, but Cuban musicologists generally agree that Orestes López was the real creator. López was a nobody. An ordinary player with a symphony orchestra who was buried under the mountain of fame heaped upon Pérez Prado.'

The interview was over but I wasn't ready to head towards the exit. Roberto's seedling had taken root: who was Pilar? What was the blood-chilling tale?

Tony cleared the coffee cups off the table. 'I've been to America and I've seen faith healers free worshippers from their pain. Dancing is our faith healer. The rumba miraculously frees us from the agony of daily life in Cuba.'

'Roberto said something scary happened to you.'

'Scary?'

'A woman named Pilar. In Santiago.' From Tony's expression I realised I'd rubbed a sensitive spot. 'I'm sorry. It's none of my business. I'm constantly looking for a good story –'

'It wasn't scary. That's the wrong word.'

'Actually, he didn't say scary. He said chilling. I shouldn't have brought it up –'

'Shocking. That's the correct word. Something shocking happened to me in Santiago. There's some coffee left. I'll heat it up and we'll sit here and I'll explain why, whenever I think of Pilar Velez, I know I'm the unluckiest man on the planet.'

He came back with hot coffee.

'This was before the Revolution, before Tía Tata and his scruffy friends marched into Havana. I was young and full of fire. I reckoned I was the best damn saxophonist in the Americas, and who can say, maybe I was. Back then I was strictly jazz – none of the hotel tourist rubbish I do now. I played regularly with Tomás Puente's quartet. He needed a singer. He was auditioning girls. Pilar walked up to the mike and I was bowled over. What a voice! How can I describe it? Similar to Billie Holiday, but her own sound, no imitation. And looks – my God, was she a looker. Long legs and good cheekbones. The smile of a goddess.

'Tomás hired somebody else, a second-rate talent. I was flabbergasted. Tomás' brother was with the quartet and he told me Tomás thought she was too good. She'd be the big star, and not him. I tracked down Pilar's address and went to encourage her to stay in music. Her mother came to the door, the vile-mouthed old bitch. I haven't forgotten her words. "I know why you want my daughter. For sex. Go pay a prostitute. Pilar's marrying money. Pilar's marrying a rich doctor."

'By chance, I bumped into Pilar at a concert. She was marrying a doctor and he was rich, but she was as drawn to me as I was to her. We slept together. Many times. Pilar married the doctor and we still slept together. We cared for each other. Pilar cared for the doctor's money but not for the doctor. Did she have a singing career? No. The doctor wouldn't permit it. Singers, dancers, actresses – in his mind they were sluts.

'Her marriage broke up. Pilar moved in with me and we were happy lovebirds. Or so I thought. Pilar's mother was obsessed with money. She walked to and from her job at the Partagás factory – miles and miles – to save the bus fare. The plumbing in her neighbour's house wasn't working so the neighbour filled a bucket in her yard, and the vile-mouthed bitch charged her for the water. Pilar wasn't that cheap, but she had inherited her mother's passion for the peso. She complained about being poor. I arranged an audition for her – her voice was her fortune – but she didn't show up. She had lost interest in singing. I came home after a session and she was gone. She had been secretly seeing a lawyer and she went to live with him in Santa Clara.

'I had girls – many, many girls – but I never forgot Pilar. No one had penetrated my heart that deeply. I played in Santa Clara for a week, filling in for an ailing musician. I hoped she'd come to the hotel but I never saw her. Last year, I was playing at a hotel here and the new manager's wife came up to me in the lobby. I had known her when Pilar and I were lovers. She said the last time she'd seen Pilar, twenty years ago, she had cut the lawyer loose and was living in Santiago.

'Thirty-five years had whipped by. Thirty-five. I was old, Pilar was old. I was willing to forgive her for running off with the lawyer. I had my cousin in Santiago locate her house. He was in the housing bureau and he pretended it was official business. She was in the suburbs and she appeared to be living alone. I took the train to Santiago. I got a haircut, put on my nicest shirt and took a taxi to her house.

'I knocked on the door and she didn't answer. I heard a radio playing in the back of the house. Classical music. I went inside. I called her name. "Pilar, don't be alarmed. It's me, Tony González." I went down the hall. She was in the kitchen. Dead. She had left a note on the table before hanging herself. She was lonely and depressed because nobody loved her. This is the reason I say I'm the unluckiest man on the planet. An hour earlier, and Pilar and I would be together today.'

chapter twenty-six

José Martí, the poet with a pistol, was born in a modest house near the main railway station. I didn't learn that until I accidentally came across his initial home while walking the streets of La Habana Vieja, entranced by cathedrals and convents, a proliferation of grand colonial works. Turning onto Calle Leonor Pérez, I spied the historical site sign above the doorway of the squat, stone and tile building, and reading it, wondered why it hadn't entered my mind that Martí may have been born in Havana and his birthplace could very well be a public shrine.

Martí's father, Mariano, and his mother, Leonor, settled in the house when they married in 1852. Both were of Spanish heritage. Mariano was from Valencia and Leonor was born in the Canary Islands. They met in Havana, and adhering to a white society custom, Mariano paid a 500-peso dowry to Leonor's family after it obtained documents assuring him her moral character and racial purity were stainless. On 28 January 1853, Leonor 'gave light', as the Spanish describe it, to José Julian Martí y Pérez in the three-room ground-floor flat. An ex-military officer and Havana policeman, Mariano took his family to Spain four years later, and returning in 1859, he ultimately accepted a low-paying civil service job to support his wife and seven children.

The house at 314 Calle Leonor Pérez was renovated and converted into a museum in the 1960s. Touring the premises, I discovered that the rooms were furnished in nineteenth-century style and that personal artefacts had been tracked down and placed on eternal exhibit, including the martyred patriot's clothing, desk and handwritten manuscripts. Interesting stuff, but none of it answered the question that had been tugging at me since I began my Cuban journey. I was yet to fathom what Miguel was driving at when he stated that to understand contemporary Cuba, I had to understand José Martí. Which Martí was he alluding to? The poet, the revolutionary or the journalist whose comments on the arts were, I had determined, as meritorious as his more frequently quoted political writings?

'Perhaps a superiority of painting over literature is that it commands reflection, study, amelioration and emotion changes,' Martí wrote. 'The pen has wings, and travels too rapidly; the brush has weight and does not fly swiftly.'

He also wrote: 'Forlorn is the man who has not felt a powerful force growing within him when gazing at a beautiful painting, with inexpressible words crowding at his throat, out of joy and sentiment. Such are the timeless laws of art that escape the legislators of the physical world.'

The Martí committing those lines to paper was sensitive and thoughtful. Martí the poet was often anguished and angry; Martí the political agitator, akin to many visionary underdogs, forceful, impatient and self-righteous. How could I meld the various components of Martí's personality and apply them to twenty-first century Cuba? Why hadn't Miguel laid it on the table for me? I had sensed his reluctance to discuss Martí and decided not to raise the subject again. His reticence appeared to parallel that of the disaffected athlete I'd spoken to in Santiago. The athlete said you had to be Cuban to comprehend Martí. Thinking of him and Miguel, I wondered if Martí was such a near-holy icon to

Cubans that giving foreigners a full-blown account of why they worshipped him would be like uncovering the Kaaba for the benefit of infidels.

Sitting in the small park next to the Martí museum, I perused my notebook. Looking at the exterior wall of a deserted building in Santiago, I had scribbled down a weather-faded chalk message, 'To Change Masters Is Not To Be Free.' When Carlota mouthed those identical words to criticise the outcome of a power battle within the local arts bureaucracy, I asked where they originated. 'With a genius,' she enthused. 'In the head of José Martí.'

It was logical to conclude that Martí was condemning dictatorships in general and Cuba's Spanish rulers in particular. More than sixty years later, underground dissidents revived the expression to protest the Batista coup that overthrew Prío. It wasn't difficult to appreciate why it was absent from the Martí quotations circulating like wrinkled currency in Castroland.

Looking in my notes, I saw a passage I had copied from a book on Latin American revolutionaries. Martí's mother fretted over his political activities and attempted to persuade him to jettison them. 'What a useless sacrifice you are making, my dear son,' Leonor said in a letter. 'There is not a solitary soul who is grateful for it. Most people attribute your sacrifice to a yearning for fame, others to expedience, and no one appreciates its true value.' In another letter, she urged him to recall the advice she had been issuing since he was a child. 'Anyone who tries to be a redeemer is crucified.'

Castro's Cuba was not the Cuba Martí would have embraced. Press censorship and the silencing of anti-government voices through imprisonment were stinging examples of how a changing master maintained oppression.

Writing today, Martí would be perceived, to echo his mother's words, as a redeemer deserving crucifixion.

Democracy was Martí's siren call. His devotion to attaining that goal for his homeland was enhanced by a saint-like belief in the necessity of establishing and retaining supreme moral and ethical standards for one's self. Martí was, historians agreed, a compassionate, honest, unselfish, genuinely sincere individual. The kind of person, I cynically believed, who would have trouble fitting into either a democratic or socialist political hierarchy.

I closed the notebook and walked back to the streets of colonial splendour.

Not long after that day, I went to the Riviera to have a final drink with Carlota and Roberto. The Malecón showplace had become grubby since it was built in the 1950s but a new management team, directed by a Spanish entrepreneur, was sprucing up the lobby and oceanview rooms and rejuvenating staff morale. Fifteen minutes past the rendezvous hour, Roberto swaggered over the hotel threshold. I hadn't grown any fonder of him in the time I'd been in the city, but for the sake of my research and Carlota's feelings, I hid my aversion.

'My mother should be here soon,' he said, seating himself in a lobby chair. 'What time's your plane leaving tonight?'

'It isn't tonight. I have two more days in Havana.'

'So why are we getting together today?'

'I'm scared of flying. If I don't drink alcohol and coffee forty-eight hours before a flight, I'm calmer. I don't eat chocolate. There's caffeine in it. Alcohol and caffeine increase anxiety.'

'That's ridiculous. You should get so drunk you don't care if you're scared.'

Roberto had come from the harbour where he had

spoken to a union official about a stevedoring job. He said it was a futile effort. A secret society, the Abakua, controlled the docks. The members staged Santería-like ceremonies (cultists were among African slaves shipped to Cuba) and were known to engage in theft, bribery and murder. Whereas the Santería religion welcomed female adherents, Abakua was strictly for males. Non-cultists did gain waterfront jobs, but only if an Abakua relative or newly initiated member wasn't applying.

'You don't fool with those guys,' Roberto said. 'Cross an *ekobio* and you wake up in the morning with a blood-soaked chicken head on your doorstep. Cross him again, you'll get a knife in the leg, or worse. Did you get everything you needed?'

'What do you mean?'

'In Cuba. Did you find out everything you wanted to find out?'

'Yes, I think so. Actually, one thing's eluded me. It's no big deal, but I wish I had the answer.' I explained the José Martí enigma to him. And I linked Miguel's reluctance to fully explore the topic with my Kaaba-infidel theory. I was talking primarily to keep the conversation between us from floundering; I really didn't expect Roberto, who by his own admission wasn't interested in Cuban writers, to do more than fling a familiar Martí quote in my direction, then shift to the subject that bedazzled him the most, himself.

'Sure, Martí's an icon. He could start a church and be elected pope,' Roberto said. 'I can't speak for Miguel, but it's dumb to think he was shutting up because you were a foreigner. We don't care what foreigners know about us. He probably didn't want to look too closely at Martí so he wouldn't have to confront the uncomfortable truth.'

'What uncomfortable truth?'

'There are Martí-isms that don't compliment the system Miguel pushes. Like the line that goes, "Arrogant and dangerous men promote socialist ideology in order to climb up in the world pretending to be frantic defenders of the forsaken whose shoulders they stand upon." I haven't seen that written on a whole lot of billboards. The Communists blind-eye the Martí-isms that don't fit their purposes.'

'OK, but I can't figure out what Miguel was getting at. I've read biographical material. I've read Martí's articles and poems and political tracts. I've read everything I've come across.'

Roberto nodded his approval. 'You were on the right road, you just didn't see the right signs. José Martí's our spiritual guide. You mention the Apostle to a Cuban and he'll know who you're talking about. Tell me what you think Martí did all his life.'

'He was a writer. He fought for independence.'

'He struggled. That's what he did. He struggled and he won. His martyrdom inspired the uprising that overthrew the Spanish. José Martí was proof positive that adversity – the suffering Cubans are now facing – can be overcome with perseverance and resolve.'

'To understand Cuba is to understand José Martí's ability to endure.'

'Exactly. He endured and triumphed, even though he died doing it. I know in my gut I'll never be in Miami. I know Cuba will always be my home. So I will endure, like everyone living here will endure, and I will win, like everyone living here will win. Despite the bad food, the bad hospitals, the lousy salaries and all the other indignities piled upon us.'

chapter twenty-seven

Winter on Queen Street. A bleak sky, frigid air, icy pavements, the threat of a crippling snowstorm later that day. Why was I living in Toronto? For that matter, why did anyone live anywhere in Canada between November and May? The entire country should be temporarily mothballed; on a merciful planet all 30 million of us would scamper to Arizona, New Mexico, Baja California, wherever there was room, wherever there was heat.

Wishing didn't make it so, and fighting a skin-scraping wind, I hurried along, past designer boutiques and crowded coffee houses to the establishment that was as much an essential service to me as the subway and regular rubbish collection: the local video store. My son had suggested I was a film addict ('Roll up your shirtsleeve, father. Show us the sprocket marks on your arm.'), and he was undeniably correct. There were few things finer on winter nights than firing up the VCR to view images of appealing climes. *Do The Right Thing* was good for sweltering urban streets, *A River Runs Through It* for sparkling streams, *Barry Lyndon* for pastoral greenery, *Swept Away* for sea and sun.

I was in the mood for hot sand. *Lawrence of Arabia* was out, so I rented another version of North African heat, *The Sheltering Sky*.

At my flat, I inserted the video in the machine and went downstairs to prepare a quiche. Jessie was due home shortly from her job, and as I worked from the flat, I cooked the weekday dinners.

The phone rang. I went into my office to answer it. A female voice shot sentences into my ear in rapid-fire Spanish. It was eight months since I had been in Cuba and I wasn't ready for a fast rendering of the language. The woman on the phone uttered two words I easily comprehended. She said Carlota and she said Toronto.

'Carlota isn't in Toronto,' I replied. 'Carlota is in Cuba.'

The woman laughed. 'I'll speak slower. Carlota isn't in Cuba. Carlota's in Canada. This is Carlota speaking.'

She was on the Prairies, flown north by the Cuban government as a member of a cultural delegation. She would be out west for two weeks and she had received official permission for ten days of 'soaking up the arts' in Toronto. Could she stay at our flat?

That night, Debra Winger and John Malkovich perspired and swatted at flies, but Jessie and I continually shut them out. Carlota's visit excited us. We'd take her to the ballet, the Art Gallery of Ontario, the Factory Theatre. She'd be overwhelmed by the number of shops at the Eaton Centre, the abundance of food at Loblaws. While John Malkovich was dying in a barren, mud-walled room, we were debating which ethnic restaurants to take Carlota to.

Carlota alighted from the train wrapped in a faded parka a Canadian friend had lent her. It was pink and trimmed with white fake fur. It came as no surprise to me that wearing the hideous coat didn't diminish Carlota's self-assurance. She strutted the marble concourse, flight bag swinging, head erect, like a diva performing in a shoddy costume.

Kissing us on the cheeks, she exclaimed, 'Crazy country! You need big heaters in the streets!'

In the taxi, Carlota brought us up to date. Roberto was in the military. He had already served his compulsory two-year term, and in returning to the service, he had told a superior officer that he was motivated by a compulsion to defend the country against the United States. (In my mind, I hadn't cast Roberto, a smug, self-centred, Miami-adoring cat snatcher, as an ardent anti-American, and cynical to the core, I silently decided his enlistment was motivated by the opportunity to enjoy three daily meals.) The news from Holguín included the item that Rosa was suffering a vitamin deficiency owing to her poor diet; Carlota's Canadian friend had bought pills and was taking them to Cuba on an upcoming holiday. As for Vicente and Nena, their wedding was on again. A niece had died and they were moving into her old room when they got married. It was roughly the same size as the backyard shed Vicente now slept in, but it was in a proper house. Icing the cake, Vicente had landed a coveted job, waiting tables in a tourist hotel, and swore he was quitting the black market. I didn't pick up on it at the time, but Carlota omitted her daughter from the gossipy summary.

For the next couple of days, Carlota unwittingly demolished some of our plans. Art galleries and plays held meagre interest and she preferred cheeseburgers, beef steak and hotdogs to ethnic dishes. She had seen many shopping malls and supermarkets in American magazines and films and she wasn't, as we had erroneously forecast, bowled over by their excessive displays of consumerism.

The cold weather limited outdoor excursions. Wearing a subtle-shaded coat of Jessie's, she took a short hurried walk each morning and attended the ballet one evening. To my delight, her greatest desire was to watch films. The VCR hummed.

Once or twice a day, she went into my office to take a phone call. Friends out west, she'd explain. Relatives in Miami. Sometimes she'd appear sombre and distant following a call, but the evidence of internal strife soon vanished. One night it didn't. We were drinking after-dinner coffee and Jessie asked if there was anything she'd like to take back to Cuba with her.

'I might not be going back,' Carlota said pointedly.

'What do you mean?' Jessie asked.

'There's a man in Miami. I want to go to him. Are there guards on the border? Can I walk across?'

'Yes, of course there are guards,' I said. 'Canadian and American customs officers. It's impossible to simply walk across. You need papers.'

Her eyes filled with tears. 'I won't cry. I've cried enough in my life.' She paused, staring at the table, and when she continued speaking, there were no tears. 'Roberto is old enough to look after himself. Delores isn't. By going to Antonio, I will be abandoning her. This is the choice, Delores or Antonio. I love them both. I can't bear the thought of living without my little girl.'

In the lift the following day, I ran into a neighbour who used to do refugee work for a Quaker organisation. She wasn't up on current immigration law, but she passed on the name of someone who was. Linda Read belonged to a Toronto-based volunteer group aiding refugees from Somalia and Latin America. Canadian law stated that in order to avert deportation, would-be immigrants must prove they were fleeing political persecution. In some cases, unable to prove that, refugees were deported to face certain imprisonment or death.

Over the phone, I told Read about Carlota's plight. She revealed that few Cubans were permitted to stay in Canada because most were fleeing for economic reasons and not persecution. Deportation was the usual outcome for attempting to cross the border illegally into the United States. I understood what deportation entailed for an arrested Cuban defector: if they weren't jailed, they'd lose their job and be hard-pressed to obtain a new one. Some defectors were forced to live off family and friends for years. Spouses and children might also be punished. Delores, for instance, wouldn't be stopped from gaining a teaching certificate, but she might find that the only position available to her would be teaching in a remote rural school where extreme hardship was the norm. Hardly any textbooks or writing paper, and students sharing the class pencil; her residence could be a dirt-floor shack with no electricity or indoor plumbing. And Roberto, regardless of how efficient he was in the military, might be permanently glued to the lower ranks.

'How can a mother choose between her child and the man she loves?' Read said, sounding genuinely sympathetic. 'The poor woman. Whatever she decides to do, she'll regret it. Have you or your wife given her any advice?'

'What kind of advice?'

'Whether or not to defect.'

'No. We're too stunned by the fact that she's considering it. She loves Cuba. She's an avid Communist.'

'Don't get deeply involved. It's against the law in Canada to counsel refugees.'

'Really? I never heard of that law.'

'Well, it exists. You and your wife shouldn't try to persuade her to defect or to return home. Say nothing. Remain neutral. That may save you some bad feelings down the line. Quite often, people do something you advised them not to do. Then you're hurt because your opinion – all the hours you spent discussing their problem – really didn't matter a great deal to them.'

No opinions, no persuasion. The middle of the road was not a route Jessie or I customarily travelled. Yet we did it. With a lot of tongue-biting difficulty.

Six days into Carlota's stay, the temperature rose. The bitterness was gone, but the air was still cold, still hostile. I took Carlota to the roof of our block of flats. The view usually impressed visitors and she was no exception. The world's longest cement slab – the CN Tower – and a cluster of downtown high-rises were sharply etched against the clear sky. The municipal airport's white, wood-frame terminal and the snow-dusted trees of the Toronto Islands lay between the harbour and Lake Ontario's massive, grey waters.

'It's beautiful,' Carlota enthused.

'Remember the night we were on your roof in Havana?' I asked. 'The air was blue. That's how I think of Cuba now. All that hardship and suffering, and I have this absurdly romantic image. Blue Cuban nights. I ought to be ashamed of myself. I see your country as an exotic dream. Food shortages, dictators, a violent history – nothing ruins its beauty, nothing destroys the Cuban spirit.'

'It is an exotic dream,' Carlota said. 'When I'm in the countryside and I see the lushness, the incredible colours, I know I'm close to paradise. But beauty isn't enough and neither is an indestructible spirit. Something else is more essential. Love between humans.'

Carlota loved her children, openly and unremittingly. But she had been anguished by a secret passion for the past sixteen years, pining for the man named Antonio. She had known him since she was fourteen. As an adolescent, she felt 'peculiar, not myself' in his presence and 'missing a wheel' when he wasn't around. He was tall, hauntingly good-looking, three years Carlota's senior, and like her, a ballet student. Unlike her, he wasn't keen on a dance career. He pursued girls as though that were his true vocation and, dropping ballet, studied law. When she was eighteen, Carlota met him on the street and they had coffee together. She lost her virginity to Antonio a few months later, on a sofa while her parents were out.

'Unfaithful,' she said, gazing at a ferry crossing the channel to the airport. 'Fidelity was a knack Antonio never acquired.'

He implored her to quit the ballet and marry him. She rejected the proposal, surmising that his womanising wouldn't end at the altar. They went their separate ways. She married Raúl and they had a son. But she always loved Antonio and they'd had brief affairs umpteen times over the years. Now Antonio was in Miami, a defector, recently divorced, writing letters begging her to come to America and marry him.

'He's middle-aged and swears he's finished with other women. None of them – not even his two wives – were as dear to him as I was. We were like twins.' She turned to me, anxiety darkening her eyes. 'Delores is Antonio's daughter. Raúl added up dates and realised she wasn't his child, which is why he ran off with The Lesbian.'

'Does Delores know Antonio's her father?'

'No. Neither does Roberto or Antonio. If I go to America, Delores will live with my mother. She will be fed and have her own room and I'll send money. But how can I leave her? She's young and pretty. My mother's old and tired and can't protect her from men. I should be there until Delores is grown and wed. I'm completely confused. The government probably won't let me outside Cuba again. This is my best chance. What should I do? Go home or go to Miami?'

'I have no idea,' I said. 'It's your decision, Carlota.'

I was lying; I did have an idea. Once a womaniser, forever a womaniser. Antonio was offering short-term ecstasy, leading to long-term distress. Go home, I thought. Go home to Delores and Roberto and some guy who doesn't screw around.

Two days afterwards, she emerged from my office and said that was the last call she would be receiving from Antonio. He wept and pleaded when she said she had decided not to join him. 'I am very upset,' she said to us, 'but I will not cry.'

When her visit ended, we escorted her to the train station. Her suitcase was packed with gifts. I had bought the drab and battered piece of luggage for her in a charity shop. At the flat, I explained how, thanks to a rock singer, I had developed my theory on the way to discourage customs' inspections. Carlota said the trick wouldn't work for Cubans: they all had drab and battered suitcases.

We helped her on to the train, traded kisses and hugs. Standing on the platform, our breath making smoky-white clouds as though fires burned in our lungs, we watched her shove the pink parka on the overhead rack, and sitting down, turn towards the window. Our final impression of Carlota was of a striking, sombre-faced woman, her arm waving slowly, like a wind-brushed Cuban palm.

A month passed. We worked, we went out for dinner, we planned a Cuban holiday.

Late one night, we were awakened by the phone. We lay listening to the message the machine was recording. The call was from Carlota. Jessie bounded up. Their conversation was brief. Carlota feared somebody was tapping the line: Cuban Counter-Intelligence, the CIA, US Immigration, Lord knows who, and she was loath to reveal specific details.

Hanging up, Jessie said Carlota wanted to tell us she hadn't returned to Cuba. She was in Miami, living with Antonio.

'I don't believe it,' I said. 'How did that happen?'

'She didn't say.'

'She couldn't have got a visa.'

'She's working in a restaurant, in the kitchen. I asked her how she liked Miami and you know what she said? "I don't."'

'Well, she has what she wanted. She wanted Antonio.'

'Yes, and she's thrilled to be with him. Antonio's playing in a salsa band. It could be years before he becomes a landed immigrant or whatever they call it in the States. There's a big backlog of Cuban applications.'

What was it Linda Read said? Poor woman. Whatever she decides, she'll regret it. Antonio was making her happy, but how many times a day did she think of her children; how often did she clench her teeth and vow, I will not cry. The refugee life in America, so different from Roberto's starry visions of motorscooters and volleyball-playing blondes, was undoubtedly adding to her regret. Recounting his exiled years in New York, José Martí wrote, 'I know the

Monster because I have lived in its lair.' Carlota was just beginning to know the Monster. Did she have the inner resources to befriend the beast and not let it destroy her?

Going back to bed, I thought of Cuba – the brown sugar soup, the patched-together cars, the crumbling homes. If anyone possessed the savvy to survive it was, I reasoned, Carlota, and all the other Cubans who, for politics, love or economic gain, had taken up residence in the Monster's lair.